50 Spanish Sweet and Chocolate Recipes for Home

By: Kelly Johnson

Table of Contents

- Tarta de Santiago (Almond Cake)
- Crema Catalana (Spanish Custard)
- Churros con Chocolate
- Flan de Huevo (Spanish Egg Flan)
- Torrijas (Spanish French Toast)
- Natillas (Spanish Custard)
- Leche Frita (Fried Milk)
- Pestiños (Honey Pastries)
- Rosquillas (Spanish Doughnuts)
- Mantecados (Spanish Shortbread)
- Polvorones (Spanish Christmas Cookies)
- Arroz con Leche (Spanish Rice Pudding)
- Bunyols (Spanish Fritters)
- Tejas (Almond Tuiles)
- Magdalenas (Spanish Muffins)
- Alfajores (Spanish Sandwich Cookies)
- Tarta de Queso (Spanish Cheesecake)
- Panellets (Marzipan Cookies)
- Torta de Aceite (Spanish Olive Oil Cake)
- Buñuelos de Viento (Spanish Wind Fritters)
- Tarta de Manzana (Spanish Apple Tart)
- Turrones (Spanish Nougat)
- Crema de Calabaza (Spanish Pumpkin Cream)
- Yemas de Santa Teresa (Spanish Egg Yolk Candies)
- Borrachuelos (Spanish Anise Cookies)
- Bizcocho de Chocolate (Spanish Chocolate Cake)
- Sopa de Fresas (Spanish Strawberry Soup)
- Crema de Chocolate (Spanish Chocolate Cream)
- Torta de Santiago (Spanish Almond Cake)
- Sobao Pasiego (Spanish Sponge Cake)
- Buñuelos de Calabaza (Spanish Pumpkin Fritters)
- Gachas Manchegas (Spanish Porridge)
- Pan de Higo (Spanish Fig Bread)
- Ensaimadas (Spanish Sweet Rolls)
- Cabello de Ángel (Angel Hair Candy)

- Huesos de Santo (Spanish Saints' Bones)
- Crema de Orujo (Spanish Cream Liqueur)
- Tarta de Melocotón (Spanish Peach Tart)
- Polvorón de Canela (Spanish Cinnamon Shortbread)
- Tejas de Almendra (Almond Tile Cookies)
- Frutas de Aragón (Spanish Fruit Candies)
- Crema de Limón (Spanish Lemon Cream)
- Tocino de Cielo (Heaven's Bacon)
- Goxua (Basque Trifle)
- Migas Extremeñas (Spanish Crumb Cake)
- Hornazo (Spanish Easter Cake)
- Pastissets (Spanish Pastry)
- Carajitos de Jerez (Spanish Almond Cookies)
- Crema de Naranja (Spanish Orange Cream)
- Empanada Gallega (Galician Sweet Pie)

Tarta de Santiago (Almond Cake)

Ingredients:

- 250g (about 2 cups) almond flour
- 200g (about 1 cup) granulated sugar
- 4 large eggs
- Zest of 1 lemon
- Zest of 1 orange
- 1 teaspoon vanilla extract
- Powdered sugar, for dusting

Instructions:

Preheat your oven to 350°F (175°C). Grease a 9-inch (23cm) round cake pan and line the bottom with parchment paper.

In a large mixing bowl, beat the eggs with the granulated sugar until light and fluffy.

Add the almond flour, lemon zest, orange zest, and vanilla extract to the egg mixture. Gently fold everything together until well combined.

Pour the batter into the prepared cake pan and spread it out evenly.

Bake in the preheated oven for about 30-35 minutes, or until the cake is golden brown on top and a toothpick inserted into the center comes out clean.

Remove the cake from the oven and let it cool in the pan for about 10 minutes. Then, carefully transfer it to a wire rack to cool completely.

Once the cake has cooled, place a stencil of the Cross of Saint James (or any desired design) on top of the cake. Dust powdered sugar over the stencil to create the pattern.

Carefully remove the stencil to reveal the design on the cake.

Slice and serve the Tarta de Santiago on its own or with a dollop of whipped cream or a scoop of vanilla ice cream.

Enjoy this deliciously simple yet elegant Spanish almond cake!

Crema Catalana (Spanish Custard)

Ingredients:

- 4 cups (1 liter) whole milk
- 1 cinnamon stick
- Zest of 1 lemon
- Zest of 1 orange
- 6 large egg yolks
- 1 cup (200g) granulated sugar, divided
- 1/4 cup (30g) cornstarch
- Additional granulated sugar for caramelizing

Instructions:

In a saucepan, combine the whole milk, cinnamon stick, lemon zest, and orange zest. Heat the mixture over medium heat until it just starts to simmer. Remove from heat and let it steep for about 10-15 minutes to infuse the flavors.

In a separate bowl, whisk together the egg yolks and half of the granulated sugar (1/2 cup) until pale and creamy.

In another small bowl, mix the cornstarch with a little bit of milk from the saucepan to create a slurry.

After the milk has steeped, remove the cinnamon stick and citrus zest, then return the saucepan to the stove over medium heat. Stir in the cornstarch slurry. Gradually pour a small amount of the hot milk mixture into the egg yolk mixture, whisking constantly to temper the eggs. Continue adding the hot milk mixture slowly while whisking until everything is well combined.

Pour the mixture back into the saucepan and cook over medium heat, stirring constantly with a wooden spoon, until the custard thickens and coats the back of the spoon. This should take about 5-7 minutes.

Remove the custard from the heat and pour it into individual serving dishes or ramekins. Let them cool to room temperature, then cover and refrigerate for at least 2 hours, or until set.

Just before serving, sprinkle a thin, even layer of granulated sugar over the top of each custard. Use a kitchen torch to caramelize the sugar until it forms a golden-brown crust. Alternatively, you can place the custards under a broiler for a few minutes until the sugar caramelizes.

Allow the caramelized sugar to cool and harden for a minute or two before serving.

Enjoy this creamy and indulgent Crema Catalana, a delightful Spanish dessert!

Churros con Chocolate

Churros Ingredients:

- 1 cup water
- 2 1/2 tablespoons granulated sugar
- 1/2 teaspoon salt
- 2 tablespoons vegetable oil
- 1 cup all-purpose flour
- Vegetable oil, for frying

Chocolate Sauce Ingredients:

- 1 cup semi-sweet chocolate chips
- 1 cup heavy cream
- 1/2 teaspoon vanilla extract
- Pinch of salt

Instructions:

Prepare the Churro Dough:
- In a saucepan, combine water, sugar, salt, and vegetable oil. Bring to a boil over medium-high heat.
- Remove from heat and stir in the flour until the mixture forms a smooth dough.
- Transfer the dough to a piping bag fitted with a star tip.

Fry the Churros:
- Heat vegetable oil in a deep frying pan or pot to 375°F (190°C).
- Pipe 4-6 inch strips of dough directly into the hot oil, using scissors to cut them from the piping bag.
- Fry the churros until golden brown, about 2-3 minutes per side.
- Remove the churros from the oil and drain them on paper towels.

Make the Chocolate Sauce:
- In a small saucepan, heat the heavy cream over medium heat until it just begins to simmer.
- Place the chocolate chips in a heatproof bowl and pour the hot cream over them. Let it sit for a minute.
- Add vanilla extract and a pinch of salt, then stir until the chocolate is melted and the mixture is smooth.

Serve:
- Serve the warm churros with the chocolate sauce for dipping.
- Optionally, sprinkle the churros with a mixture of cinnamon and sugar before serving.

Enjoy these crispy, golden churros dipped in rich and creamy chocolate sauce! Perfect for a sweet treat any time of day.

Flan de Huevo (Spanish Egg Flan)

Ingredients:

For the caramel:

- 1 cup (200g) granulated sugar
- 1/4 cup water

For the flan:

- 4 large eggs
- 2 cups (480ml) whole milk
- 1 teaspoon vanilla extract
- 1/2 cup (100g) granulated sugar

Instructions:

    Prepare the Caramel:
- In a small saucepan, combine the granulated sugar and water over medium heat.
- Stir continuously until the sugar dissolves.
- Once the sugar has dissolved, stop stirring and allow the mixture to simmer until it turns a deep golden brown color, swirling the pan occasionally to ensure even caramelization.
- Remove from heat and immediately pour the caramel into the bottom of a flan mold or individual ramekins, swirling to coat the bottom evenly. Be careful as the caramel will be very hot. Set aside to cool and harden.

    Prepare the Flan Mixture:
- Preheat your oven to 350°F (175°C).
- In a mixing bowl, whisk together the eggs, whole milk, vanilla extract, and granulated sugar until well combined and smooth.

    Assemble and Bake:
- Pour the flan mixture over the cooled caramel in the flan mold or ramekins.
- Place the flan mold or ramekins into a larger baking dish. Fill the larger dish with hot water until it reaches about halfway up the sides of the flan mold or ramekins, creating a water bath.

- Carefully transfer the baking dish to the preheated oven and bake for 45-55 minutes, or until the flan is set around the edges but still slightly jiggly in the center.
- Once baked, remove the flan from the oven and allow it to cool to room temperature. Then, cover and refrigerate for at least 4 hours, or preferably overnight, to chill and set completely.

Serve:
- To serve, run a knife around the edge of the flan mold or ramekins to loosen the flan.
- Place a serving plate upside down over the mold or ramekin, then quickly and carefully flip it over to release the flan onto the plate, allowing the caramel to flow over the top.
- Slice and serve the flan cold, either on its own or with whipped cream or fresh fruit, if desired.

Enjoy this creamy and decadent Spanish egg flan, a classic dessert that's sure to impress!

Torrijas (Spanish French Toast)

Ingredients:

- 1 loaf of stale bread (preferably a day or two old), cut into thick slices
- 4 cups (960ml) whole milk
- 1 cinnamon stick
- Zest of 1 lemon
- Zest of 1 orange
- 4 large eggs
- 1 cup (200g) granulated sugar
- Vegetable oil, for frying
- Ground cinnamon, for sprinkling (optional)
- Honey or syrup, for drizzling (optional)

Instructions:

Prepare the Milk Mixture:
- In a saucepan, combine the whole milk, cinnamon stick, lemon zest, and orange zest. Heat the mixture over medium heat until it just starts to simmer. Remove from heat and let it cool slightly.

Soak the Bread:
- In a shallow dish, whisk the eggs together with half of the granulated sugar (1/2 cup).
- Dip each slice of bread into the milk mixture, making sure to soak both sides well but not to let it become too soggy.
- Then, dip the soaked bread slices into the egg mixture, coating them evenly.

Fry the Torrijas:
- Heat vegetable oil in a large frying pan over medium heat.
- Once the oil is hot, carefully place the soaked bread slices into the pan in batches, being careful not to overcrowd the pan.
- Fry the torrijas until golden brown and crispy on both sides, about 2-3 minutes per side.
- Remove the torrijas from the oil and drain them on paper towels to remove excess oil.

Coat with Sugar:

- While the torrijas are still warm, sprinkle them with the remaining granulated sugar (1/2 cup) on both sides, coating them evenly.
- Optionally, sprinkle ground cinnamon over the torrijas for extra flavor.

Serve:
- Serve the torrijas warm or at room temperature.
- Drizzle with honey or syrup, if desired, before serving.

Enjoy these deliciously sweet and cinnamon-infused Spanish torrijas, perfect for breakfast, brunch, or dessert!

Natillas (Spanish Custard)

Ingredients:

- 4 cups (960ml) whole milk
- 1 cinnamon stick
- Zest of 1 lemon
- Zest of 1 orange
- 6 large egg yolks
- 1/2 cup (100g) granulated sugar
- 2 tablespoons cornstarch
- Ground cinnamon, for garnish (optional)

Instructions:

Prepare the Milk Mixture:
- In a saucepan, combine the whole milk, cinnamon stick, lemon zest, and orange zest. Heat the mixture over medium heat until it just starts to simmer. Remove from heat and let it steep for about 10-15 minutes to infuse the flavors.

Whisk Egg Yolks:
- In a mixing bowl, whisk together the egg yolks and granulated sugar until pale and creamy.

Thicken the Custard:
- In a small bowl, dissolve the cornstarch in a little bit of milk from the saucepan to create a slurry.
- Gradually pour a small amount of the hot milk mixture into the egg yolk mixture, whisking constantly to temper the eggs.
- Then, whisk in the cornstarch slurry until well combined.
- Pour the egg mixture back into the saucepan with the remaining milk mixture.

Cook the Custard:
- Place the saucepan back on the stove over medium heat. Cook the mixture, stirring constantly with a wooden spoon, until it thickens and coats the back of the spoon, about 5-7 minutes. Be careful not to let it boil.

Chill and Serve:
- Once the custard has thickened, remove it from the heat and strain it through a fine mesh sieve to remove the cinnamon stick and citrus zest.
- Divide the custard among individual serving dishes or ramekins.

- Let the natillas cool to room temperature, then cover and refrigerate for at least 2 hours, or until chilled and set.

Garnish and Serve:
- Before serving, optionally sprinkle ground cinnamon over the top of each natilla for garnish.
- Serve the natillas cold, either on their own or with a sprinkle of cinnamon on top.

Enjoy this smooth and creamy Spanish custard as a delightful dessert or sweet treat!

Leche Frita (Fried Milk)

Ingredients:

- 4 cups (960ml) whole milk
- 1 cinnamon stick
- Zest of 1 lemon
- Zest of 1 orange
- 1 cup (200g) granulated sugar
- 1/2 cup (60g) cornstarch
- 3 large egg yolks
- Vegetable oil, for frying
- All-purpose flour, for dredging
- 2 large eggs, beaten
- Bread crumbs, for coating
- Powdered sugar, for dusting
- Ground cinnamon, for garnish (optional)

Instructions:

Prepare the Milk Mixture:
- In a saucepan, combine the whole milk, cinnamon stick, lemon zest, and orange zest. Heat the mixture over medium heat until it just starts to simmer. Remove from heat and let it steep for about 10-15 minutes to infuse the flavors.

Make the Custard Base:
- In a separate bowl, whisk together the granulated sugar and cornstarch.
- Gradually add a small amount of the hot milk mixture to the sugar-cornstarch mixture, whisking constantly to prevent lumps.
- Once combined, pour the mixture back into the saucepan with the remaining milk mixture.

Cook the Custard:
- Place the saucepan back on the stove over medium heat. Cook the mixture, stirring constantly with a wooden spoon, until it thickens and resembles a custard, about 5-7 minutes.
- Remove the saucepan from the heat and stir in the egg yolks until well incorporated.

- Pour the custard into a shallow dish or baking pan lined with parchment paper. Smooth the top with a spatula and let it cool to room temperature. Once cooled, cover and refrigerate for at least 2 hours, or until set and firm.

Prepare for Frying:
- Once the custard is chilled and firm, remove it from the refrigerator and cut it into desired shapes, such as squares or rectangles.
- Set up a dredging station with three separate bowls: one with all-purpose flour, one with beaten eggs, and one with bread crumbs.

Fry the Leche Frita:
- Heat vegetable oil in a deep frying pan or pot to 350°F (175°C).
- Dredge each piece of chilled custard first in the flour, then dip it into the beaten eggs, and finally coat it thoroughly with bread crumbs.
- Carefully place the coated custard pieces into the hot oil and fry until golden brown and crispy on all sides, about 1-2 minutes per side.
- Once fried, remove the Leche Frita from the oil using a slotted spoon and drain them on paper towels to remove excess oil.

Serve:
- Arrange the fried custard pieces on a serving platter and dust them generously with powdered sugar.
- Optionally, sprinkle ground cinnamon over the top for extra flavor.
- Serve the Leche Frita warm as a delightful dessert or sweet snack.

Enjoy the crispy and creamy goodness of Leche Frita, a beloved Spanish treat!

Pestiños (Honey Pastries)

Ingredients:

For the Dough:

- 4 cups (500g) all-purpose flour
- 1/2 cup (100g) granulated sugar
- 1 teaspoon ground cinnamon
- Zest of 1 orange
- Zest of 1 lemon
- Pinch of salt
- 1/2 cup (120ml) dry white wine
- 1/2 cup (120ml) olive oil or vegetable oil

For Frying:

- Vegetable oil, for frying

For the Honey Syrup:

- 1 cup (240ml) honey
- 1/2 cup (120ml) water
- 1 cinnamon stick
- Zest of 1 lemon
- Zest of 1 orange

Instructions:

Prepare the Dough:
- In a large mixing bowl, combine the all-purpose flour, granulated sugar, ground cinnamon, orange zest, lemon zest, and a pinch of salt.
- Gradually add the dry white wine and olive oil, mixing until a dough forms. Knead the dough on a lightly floured surface until smooth and elastic.

Shape the Dough:
- Divide the dough into small portions and roll each portion into a thin rectangle, about 1/8 inch (3mm) thick.

- Using a pastry cutter or knife, cut the rectangles into diamond shapes or squares. You can also use a cookie cutter for different shapes if desired.

Fry the Pestiños:
- Heat vegetable oil in a deep frying pan or pot to 350°F (175°C).
- Carefully place the shaped dough pieces into the hot oil, frying them in batches until golden brown and crispy on both sides, about 2-3 minutes per side.
- Once fried, remove the pestiños from the oil using a slotted spoon and drain them on paper towels to remove excess oil.

Make the Honey Syrup:
- In a separate saucepan, combine the honey, water, cinnamon stick, lemon zest, and orange zest. Heat the mixture over medium heat, stirring occasionally, until it comes to a simmer.
- Let the syrup simmer for about 5 minutes to thicken slightly, then remove it from the heat and let it cool slightly.

Coat the Pestiños:
- While the syrup is still warm, dip each fried pestiño into the honey syrup, coating it thoroughly.
- Place the coated pestiños on a wire rack set over a baking sheet to allow any excess syrup to drip off.

Serve:
- Let the pestiños cool completely before serving.
- Enjoy these delicious honey pastries as a sweet treat with a cup of coffee or tea, or as part of a festive dessert spread.

These Pestiños are sure to be a hit with family and friends, bringing a taste of Spanish tradition to your table!

Rosquillas (Spanish Doughnuts)

Ingredients:

For the Dough:

- 3 cups (375g) all-purpose flour
- 1 tablespoon baking powder
- 1/4 teaspoon salt
- 1/2 cup (100g) granulated sugar
- Zest of 1 lemon
- 2 large eggs
- 1/4 cup (60ml) milk
- 1/4 cup (60ml) olive oil or vegetable oil
- 1/2 teaspoon vanilla extract

For Frying:

- Vegetable oil, for frying

For the Glaze:

- 1 cup (120g) powdered sugar
- 2-3 tablespoons milk
- 1/2 teaspoon vanilla extract

Instructions:

Prepare the Dough:
- In a large mixing bowl, whisk together the all-purpose flour, baking powder, salt, granulated sugar, and lemon zest.
- In a separate bowl, beat the eggs. Then, add the milk, olive oil, and vanilla extract, and whisk until well combined.
- Gradually pour the wet ingredients into the dry ingredients, stirring until a soft dough forms. If the dough is too sticky, add a little more flour; if it's too dry, add a little more milk.

Shape the Doughnuts:
- On a lightly floured surface, roll out the dough to about 1/2 inch (1.3cm) thickness.

- Use a doughnut cutter or two different sized round cookie cutters to cut out doughnut shapes. You can also shape them by hand if preferred.

Fry the Rosquillas:
- Heat vegetable oil in a deep frying pan or pot to 350°F (175°C).
- Carefully place the shaped doughnuts into the hot oil, frying them in batches until golden brown on both sides, about 2-3 minutes per side.
- Once fried, remove the rosquillas from the oil using a slotted spoon and drain them on paper towels to remove excess oil.

Make the Glaze:
- In a small bowl, whisk together the powdered sugar, milk, and vanilla extract until smooth. Adjust the consistency by adding more milk if needed.

Glaze the Rosquillas:
- Dip each fried rosquilla into the glaze, coating it evenly. You can also drizzle the glaze over the rosquillas using a spoon.

Serve:
- Let the glazed rosquillas sit for a few minutes to allow the glaze to set.
- Enjoy these delicious Spanish doughnuts as a sweet snack or dessert with your favorite hot beverage.

These Rosquillas are sure to delight your taste buds with their fluffy texture and sweet glaze, making them a perfect treat for any occasion!

Mantecados (Spanish Shortbread)

Ingredients:

- 2 cups (250g) all-purpose flour
- 1 cup (200g) granulated sugar
- 1 cup (225g) lard or vegetable shortening
- 1 teaspoon ground cinnamon
- Zest of 1 lemon
- Zest of 1 orange
- Powdered sugar, for dusting

Instructions:

Prepare the Dough:
- In a large mixing bowl, combine the all-purpose flour, granulated sugar, ground cinnamon, lemon zest, and orange zest.
- Add the lard or vegetable shortening to the dry ingredients, and mix with your hands or a pastry cutter until the mixture resembles coarse crumbs and starts to come together into a dough.

Shape the Mantecados:
- Preheat your oven to 350°F (175°C) and line a baking sheet with parchment paper.
- Take small portions of the dough and roll them into balls, about 1 inch (2.5cm) in diameter. Then, flatten each ball slightly to form a disc shape.
- Place the shaped mantecados on the prepared baking sheet, leaving a little space between each one.

Bake the Mantecados:
- Bake the mantecados in the preheated oven for 15-20 minutes, or until they are lightly golden around the edges.
- Remove the baking sheet from the oven and let the mantecados cool for a few minutes before transferring them to a wire rack to cool completely.

Dust with Powdered Sugar:
- Once the mantecados have cooled completely, dust them generously with powdered sugar. You can do this by placing some powdered sugar in a fine mesh sieve and gently tapping it over the cookies to create an even coating.

Serve:

- Arrange the dusted mantecados on a serving platter and enjoy them with your favorite hot beverage or as a sweet snack.

These Mantecados are a delightful treat that captures the essence of Spanish cuisine, perfect for sharing with family and friends during the holiday season or any special occasion.

Polvorones (Spanish Christmas Cookies)

Ingredients:

- 2 cups (250g) all-purpose flour
- 1 cup (125g) ground almonds (or almond flour)
- 1 cup (225g) unsalted butter, at room temperature
- 1/2 cup (100g) granulated sugar
- 1 teaspoon ground cinnamon
- 1/4 teaspoon ground cloves
- 1/4 teaspoon salt
- Powdered sugar, for dusting

Instructions:

Prepare the Dough:
- Preheat your oven to 350°F (175°C) and line a baking sheet with parchment paper.
- In a large mixing bowl, combine the all-purpose flour, ground almonds, granulated sugar, ground cinnamon, ground cloves, and salt.
- Add the unsalted butter to the dry ingredients, and mix with your hands or a pastry cutter until the mixture resembles coarse crumbs and starts to come together into a dough.

Shape the Polvorones:
- Take portions of the dough and shape them into small rounds or discs, about 1 inch (2.5cm) in diameter and 1/2 inch (1.3cm) thick. You can also use cookie cutters for different shapes if desired.
- Place the shaped polvorones on the prepared baking sheet, leaving a little space between each one.

Bake the Polvorones:
- Bake the polvorones in the preheated oven for 12-15 minutes, or until they are lightly golden around the edges.
- Remove the baking sheet from the oven and let the polvorones cool for a few minutes before transferring them to a wire rack to cool completely.

Dust with Powdered Sugar:
- Once the polvorones have cooled completely, dust them generously with powdered sugar. You can do this by placing some powdered sugar in a fine mesh sieve and gently tapping it over the cookies to create an even coating.

Serve:
- Arrange the dusted polvorones on a serving platter and enjoy them with a cup of coffee, tea, or hot chocolate.

These Polvorones are a delightful addition to any holiday cookie platter or festive gathering, capturing the flavors of Spanish Christmas traditions with every crumbly bite.

Arroz con Leche (Spanish Rice Pudding)

Ingredients:

- 1 cup (200g) white rice (short or medium grain)
- 4 cups (960ml) whole milk
- 1 cinnamon stick
- Zest of 1 lemon
- Zest of 1 orange
- 1/2 cup (100g) granulated sugar (adjust to taste)
- 1/4 teaspoon salt
- 1 teaspoon vanilla extract
- Ground cinnamon, for garnish (optional)

Instructions:

Prepare the Rice:
- Rinse the rice under cold water until the water runs clear. This helps remove excess starch and prevents the rice from becoming too sticky.
- In a large saucepan, combine the rinsed rice with 2 cups (480ml) of water. Bring to a boil over medium-high heat, then reduce the heat to low and simmer, covered, for about 15-20 minutes, or until the rice is cooked and most of the water is absorbed.

Make the Rice Pudding:
- Once the rice is cooked, add the whole milk to the saucepan along with the cinnamon stick, lemon zest, and orange zest.
- Stir in the granulated sugar and salt. Bring the mixture to a gentle simmer over medium heat, stirring occasionally to prevent the rice from sticking to the bottom of the pan.
- Continue to cook the rice pudding, stirring occasionally, for about 20-25 minutes, or until the mixture thickens and the rice is soft and creamy.

Add Flavorings:
- Remove the saucepan from the heat and discard the cinnamon stick, lemon zest, and orange zest.
- Stir in the vanilla extract, adjusting the sweetness to taste by adding more sugar if desired.

Chill and Serve:
- Transfer the rice pudding to serving bowls or individual ramekins.

- Cover the bowls with plastic wrap, making sure the wrap touches the surface of the pudding to prevent a skin from forming.
- Refrigerate the rice pudding for at least 2 hours, or until chilled and set.

Garnish and Serve:
- Before serving, sprinkle ground cinnamon over the top of each bowl for garnish, if desired.
- Serve the Arroz con Leche cold as a deliciously creamy and comforting dessert.

Enjoy this classic Spanish Rice Pudding with its comforting flavors of cinnamon, citrus, and vanilla—a perfect sweet treat for any occasion!

Bunyols (Spanish Fritters)

Ingredients:

- 1 cup (240ml) water
- 1/2 cup (113g) unsalted butter
- 1/4 teaspoon salt
- 1 cup (125g) all-purpose flour
- 4 large eggs
- Zest of 1 orange
- Vegetable oil, for frying
- Powdered sugar, for dusting

Instructions:

Prepare the Dough:
- In a medium saucepan, combine the water, butter, and salt. Heat over medium heat until the butter is melted and the mixture comes to a boil.
- Reduce the heat to low, and add the flour all at once. Stir vigorously with a wooden spoon until the mixture forms a smooth dough and pulls away from the sides of the pan. This should take about 1-2 minutes.

Add Eggs and Orange Zest:
- Remove the saucepan from the heat and let the dough cool slightly.
- Once cooled, add the eggs, one at a time, beating well after each addition until fully incorporated. The dough should be smooth and glossy.
- Stir in the orange zest until evenly distributed throughout the dough.

Fry the Bunyols:
- In a deep frying pan or pot, heat vegetable oil to 350°F (175°C).
- Using two spoons or a small cookie scoop, drop spoonfuls of dough into the hot oil, working in batches to avoid overcrowding.
- Fry the bunyols until they are golden brown and puffed up, about 2-3 minutes per side.

Drain and Dust with Sugar:
- Once fried, use a slotted spoon to remove the bunyols from the oil and drain them on paper towels to remove excess oil.
- While still warm, dust the bunyols generously with powdered sugar.

Serve:

- Serve the bunyols warm as a delicious snack or dessert. They are best enjoyed fresh on the day they are made.

These Bunyols are sure to delight with their crispy exterior and soft, fluffy interior, making them a perfect treat for any special occasion or celebration. Enjoy their irresistible aroma and flavor with friends and family!

Tejas (Almond Tuiles)

Ingredients:

- 1/2 cup (113g) unsalted butter, softened
- 3/4 cup (150g) granulated sugar
- 1 teaspoon vanilla extract
- 2 large egg whites
- 1 cup (100g) almond flour or finely ground almonds
- 1/4 cup (30g) all-purpose flour
- Pinch of salt
- Sliced almonds or whole almonds, for garnish (optional)

Instructions:

Prepare the Batter:
- In a mixing bowl, cream together the softened butter, granulated sugar, and vanilla extract until light and fluffy.
- Add the egg whites, one at a time, beating well after each addition until fully incorporated.

Add Dry Ingredients:
- Gradually add the almond flour, all-purpose flour, and a pinch of salt to the batter, stirring until well combined and smooth.

Chill the Dough:
- Cover the bowl with plastic wrap and refrigerate the dough for at least 1 hour, or until firm. Chilling the dough will make it easier to handle and shape.

Shape the Tejas:
- Preheat your oven to 350°F (175°C) and line a baking sheet with parchment paper.
- Drop teaspoonfuls of the chilled dough onto the prepared baking sheet, spacing them about 2 inches (5cm) apart. Flatten each mound of dough slightly with the back of a spoon or your fingers.

Garnish (Optional):
- If desired, press a few sliced almonds or a whole almond onto each flattened mound of dough for decoration.

Bake:
- Bake the tejas in the preheated oven for 8-10 minutes, or until the edges are golden brown and the cookies are firm to the touch.

- Keep a close eye on them, as they can quickly over-brown.

Shape the Tejas:
- While still warm, use a spatula to carefully lift each cookie from the baking sheet and drape it over a rolling pin or the handle of a wooden spoon to create a curved shape. Alternatively, you can leave them flat if you prefer.

Cool and Serve:
- Allow the tejas to cool completely on a wire rack before serving.
- Store the cooled cookies in an airtight container at room temperature for up to 1 week.

Enjoy these delicate and crispy Tejas as a delightful accompaniment to tea or coffee, or as a sweet treat on their own. Their almond flavor and delicate texture make them a perfect addition to any dessert spread.

Magdalenas (Spanish Muffins)

Ingredients:

- 2 large eggs
- 1 cup (200g) granulated sugar
- 1 cup (240ml) vegetable oil or melted butter
- 1/2 cup (120ml) whole milk
- Zest of 1 lemon
- 2 cups (250g) all-purpose flour
- 2 teaspoons baking powder
- Pinch of salt
- Powdered sugar, for dusting (optional)

Instructions:

Preheat the Oven:
- Preheat your oven to 375°F (190°C). Line a muffin tin with paper liners or grease the muffin cups with butter or oil.

Beat Eggs and Sugar:
- In a large mixing bowl, beat the eggs and granulated sugar together until pale and fluffy.

Add Oil, Milk, and Lemon Zest:
- Gradually add the vegetable oil or melted butter while continuing to beat the mixture.
- Mix in the whole milk and lemon zest until well combined.

Sift Dry Ingredients:
- In a separate bowl, sift together the all-purpose flour, baking powder, and salt.

Combine Wet and Dry Ingredients:
- Gradually add the dry ingredients to the wet ingredients, mixing until just combined. Be careful not to overmix, as this can result in dense muffins.

Fill Muffin Cups:
- Spoon the batter into the prepared muffin cups, filling each one about two-thirds full.

Bake:

- Bake the magdalenas in the preheated oven for 15-20 minutes, or until they are golden brown on top and a toothpick inserted into the center comes out clean.

Cool and Serve:
- Remove the muffins from the oven and allow them to cool in the muffin tin for a few minutes before transferring them to a wire rack to cool completely.
- Once cooled, dust the magdalenas with powdered sugar, if desired, before serving.

Enjoy these delightful Spanish muffins warm or at room temperature, with your favorite hot beverage for a tasty and comforting treat!

Alfajores (Spanish Sandwich Cookies)

Ingredients:

For the Cookies:

- 1 cup (225g) unsalted butter, at room temperature
- 1/2 cup (100g) granulated sugar
- 2 large egg yolks
- 1 teaspoon vanilla extract
- 2 cups (250g) all-purpose flour
- 1/2 cup (60g) cornstarch
- 1/2 teaspoon baking powder
- Pinch of salt

For the Filling:

- Dulce de leche (store-bought or homemade)

For Dusting:

- Powdered sugar

Instructions:

Prepare the Dough:
- In a large mixing bowl, cream together the unsalted butter and granulated sugar until light and fluffy.
- Add the egg yolks and vanilla extract, and beat until well combined.

Add Dry Ingredients:
- In a separate bowl, sift together the all-purpose flour, cornstarch, baking powder, and salt.
- Gradually add the dry ingredients to the butter mixture, mixing until a soft dough forms.

Chill the Dough:
- Divide the dough into two equal portions and shape each portion into a disk.

- Wrap the disks in plastic wrap and refrigerate for at least 30 minutes, or until firm.

Roll and Cut the Cookies:
- Preheat your oven to 350°F (175°C). Line a baking sheet with parchment paper.
- On a lightly floured surface, roll out one disk of dough to about 1/4 inch (6mm) thickness.
- Use a round cookie cutter to cut out cookies. Re-roll the scraps and continue cutting until all the dough is used.
- Place the cookies on the prepared baking sheet, spacing them about 1 inch (2.5cm) apart.

Bake:
- Bake the cookies in the preheated oven for 10-12 minutes, or until the edges are lightly golden.
- Remove from the oven and let the cookies cool on the baking sheet for a few minutes before transferring them to a wire rack to cool completely.

Assemble the Alfajores:
- Once the cookies are completely cooled, spread a layer of dulce de leche on the bottom side of half of the cookies.
- Top each dulce de leche-coated cookie with another cookie to form a sandwich.

Dust with Powdered Sugar:
- Dust the tops of the alfajores with powdered sugar.

Serve:
- Serve the alfajores as a delicious sweet treat, and enjoy!

These Alfajores are sure to delight with their buttery cookies and creamy dulce de leche filling. They're perfect for enjoying with a cup of coffee or tea, or for sharing with friends and family on special occasions.

Tarta de Queso (Spanish Cheesecake)

Ingredients:

For the Crust:

- 1 1/2 cups (150g) graham cracker crumbs (or digestive biscuits)
- 1/4 cup (50g) granulated sugar
- 1/2 cup (115g) unsalted butter, melted

For the Filling:

- 24 oz (680g) cream cheese, at room temperature
- 1 cup (200g) granulated sugar
- 4 large eggs
- 1/4 cup (60ml) sour cream (or Greek yogurt)
- 1 teaspoon vanilla extract
- Zest of 1 lemon
- Pinch of salt

Instructions:

Preheat the Oven:
- Preheat your oven to 325°F (160°C). Grease a 9-inch (23cm) springform pan and line the bottom with parchment paper.

Make the Crust:
- In a mixing bowl, combine the graham cracker crumbs, granulated sugar, and melted butter until the mixture resembles wet sand.
- Press the mixture firmly into the bottom of the prepared springform pan, using the back of a spoon or your fingers to create an even layer. Set aside.

Prepare the Filling:
- In a large mixing bowl, beat the cream cheese and granulated sugar together until smooth and creamy.
- Add the eggs one at a time, beating well after each addition.
- Stir in the sour cream (or Greek yogurt), vanilla extract, lemon zest, and a pinch of salt until well combined and smooth.

Pour and Bake:
- Pour the filling over the prepared crust in the springform pan, smoothing the top with a spatula.
- Tap the pan gently on the counter to release any air bubbles.
- Place the pan on a baking sheet to catch any drips, and bake in the preheated oven for 45-55 minutes, or until the cheesecake is set around the edges but slightly jiggly in the center.

Cool and Chill:
- Remove the cheesecake from the oven and let it cool completely in the pan on a wire rack.
- Once cooled, refrigerate the cheesecake for at least 4 hours, or overnight, until firm.

Serve:
- Before serving, run a knife around the edges of the cheesecake to loosen it from the pan.
- Release the sides of the springform pan and transfer the cheesecake to a serving plate.
- Slice and serve the Tarta de Queso chilled, optionally garnished with fresh berries or a dusting of powdered sugar.

Enjoy this creamy and indulgent Spanish Cheesecake as a decadent dessert to share with friends and family on any occasion!

Panellets (Marzipan Cookies)

Ingredients:

- 1 lb (450g) almond paste or marzipan
- 1 cup (200g) granulated sugar
- 2 large egg yolks
- 1 teaspoon vanilla extract
- 1 cup (150g) pine nuts
- Additional granulated sugar, for coating (optional)
- Whole almonds, for decoration (optional)

Instructions:

Prepare the Dough:
- In a large mixing bowl, crumble the almond paste or marzipan into small pieces.
- Add the granulated sugar, egg yolks, and vanilla extract to the almond paste, and mix until well combined and the dough comes together. You may need to use your hands to knead the mixture into a smooth dough.

Shape the Panellets:
- Preheat your oven to 350°F (175°C) and line a baking sheet with parchment paper.
- Pinch off small portions of the dough and roll them into balls, about 1 inch (2.5cm) in diameter.
- Roll each ball in pine nuts, pressing the nuts gently into the dough to adhere. Alternatively, you can roll the balls in granulated sugar for a sweet coating.
- If desired, press a whole almond into the center of each panellet for decoration.

Bake the Panellets:
- Place the shaped panellets on the prepared baking sheet, spacing them about 1 inch (2.5cm) apart.
- Bake in the preheated oven for 10-12 minutes, or until the panellets are lightly golden brown around the edges.

Cool and Serve:
- Remove the panellets from the oven and let them cool on the baking sheet for a few minutes.
- Transfer the panellets to a wire rack to cool completely before serving.

Serve and Enjoy:
- Serve the panellets as a delightful sweet treat alongside coffee, tea, or hot chocolate.
- Store any leftover panellets in an airtight container at room temperature for up to several days.

These Panellets are sure to be a hit with their rich almond flavor and crunchy pine nut coating, making them a perfect addition to your holiday dessert table or any special occasion throughout the year.

Torta de Aceite (Spanish Olive Oil Cake)

Ingredients:

- 1 1/2 cups (180g) all-purpose flour
- 1 teaspoon baking powder
- 1/2 teaspoon baking soda
- 1/2 teaspoon ground cinnamon
- 1/4 teaspoon ground nutmeg
- 1/4 teaspoon salt
- 2 large eggs
- 3/4 cup (150g) granulated sugar
- 1/2 cup (120ml) extra virgin olive oil
- 1/2 cup (120ml) whole milk
- Zest of 1 orange
- Zest of 1 lemon
- 1 tablespoon orange juice
- 1 tablespoon lemon juice
- 1/2 teaspoon vanilla extract
- Powdered sugar, for dusting

Instructions:

Preheat the Oven:
- Preheat your oven to 350°F (175°C). Grease a 9-inch (23cm) round cake pan and line the bottom with parchment paper.

Prepare the Dry Ingredients:
- In a mixing bowl, sift together the all-purpose flour, baking powder, baking soda, ground cinnamon, ground nutmeg, and salt. Set aside.

Whisk the Wet Ingredients:
- In another mixing bowl, whisk together the eggs and granulated sugar until pale and slightly thickened.
- Gradually whisk in the extra virgin olive oil, followed by the whole milk, orange zest, lemon zest, orange juice, lemon juice, and vanilla extract.

Combine Wet and Dry Ingredients:
- Gradually add the dry ingredients to the wet ingredients, stirring until just combined and no lumps remain. Be careful not to overmix.

Bake the Cake:

- Pour the batter into the prepared cake pan and spread it out evenly.
- Bake in the preheated oven for 25-30 minutes, or until a toothpick inserted into the center of the cake comes out clean.

Cool and Dust with Powdered Sugar:
- Remove the cake from the oven and let it cool in the pan for about 10 minutes.
- Transfer the cake to a wire rack to cool completely.
- Once cooled, dust the top of the cake with powdered sugar for a decorative finish.

Serve and Enjoy:
- Slice the Torta de Aceite and serve it as a delightful dessert or snack, accompanied by a cup of coffee or tea.
- Store any leftovers in an airtight container at room temperature for up to several days.

With its unique combination of flavors and moist texture, this Torta de Aceite is sure to impress your taste buds and become a favorite in your repertoire of dessert recipes.

Buñuelos de Viento (Spanish Wind Fritters)

Ingredients:

- 1 cup (125g) all-purpose flour
- 1 cup (240ml) water or milk
- 4 tablespoons (50g) unsalted butter
- 1 tablespoon granulated sugar
- Pinch of salt
- 4 large eggs
- Vegetable oil, for frying
- Powdered sugar, for dusting

Instructions:

Prepare the Batter:
- In a saucepan, combine the water (or milk), unsalted butter, granulated sugar, and a pinch of salt. Heat over medium heat until the butter has melted and the mixture comes to a gentle boil.
- Reduce the heat to low and add the all-purpose flour all at once. Stir vigorously with a wooden spoon until the mixture forms a smooth dough and pulls away from the sides of the pan. This should take about 1-2 minutes.
- Remove the saucepan from the heat and let the dough cool for a few minutes.

Add Eggs:
- Once the dough has cooled slightly, add the eggs one at a time, beating well after each addition until fully incorporated. The dough should be smooth and glossy.

Fry the Buñuelos:
- In a deep frying pan or pot, heat vegetable oil over medium-high heat until it reaches 350°F (175°C).
- Drop spoonfuls of the dough into the hot oil, working in batches to avoid overcrowding. You can use two spoons to shape the dough into oval or round shapes.
- Fry the buñuelos for about 3-4 minutes, turning them occasionally, until they are golden brown and puffed up.

Drain and Dust with Powdered Sugar:

- Once fried, use a slotted spoon to remove the buñuelos from the oil and drain them on paper towels to remove excess oil.
- While still warm, dust the buñuelos generously with powdered sugar.

Serve:
- Serve the Buñuelos de Viento warm as a delicious sweet snack or dessert.
- Enjoy them with a cup of hot chocolate, coffee, or your favorite dipping sauce.

These Buñuelos de Viento are sure to delight with their light and airy texture and sweet powdered sugar coating, making them a perfect treat for any occasion!

Tarta de Manzana (Spanish Apple Tart)

Ingredients:

For the Tart Crust:

- 1 1/4 cups (150g) all-purpose flour
- 1/4 cup (50g) granulated sugar
- 1/2 cup (115g) unsalted butter, cold and cut into small pieces
- 1 large egg yolk
- 1-2 tablespoons cold water (if needed)

For the Apple Filling:

- 3-4 large apples (such as Granny Smith or Fuji), peeled, cored, and thinly sliced
- 1/4 cup (50g) granulated sugar
- 1 teaspoon ground cinnamon
- Juice of 1/2 lemon
- Zest of 1/2 lemon
- 2 tablespoons apricot jam or apple jelly, for glazing

Instructions:

Prepare the Tart Crust:
- In a large mixing bowl, combine the all-purpose flour and granulated sugar.
- Add the cold butter pieces to the flour mixture and use your fingertips or a pastry cutter to cut the butter into the flour until the mixture resembles coarse crumbs.
- Add the egg yolk and mix until the dough comes together. If the dough seems too dry, add 1-2 tablespoons of cold water, one tablespoon at a time, until the dough forms a smooth ball.
- Flatten the dough into a disk, wrap it in plastic wrap, and refrigerate for at least 30 minutes.

Preheat the Oven:
- Preheat your oven to 375°F (190°C). Lightly grease a 9-inch (23cm) tart pan with a removable bottom.

Roll Out the Dough:
- On a lightly floured surface, roll out the chilled dough into a circle slightly larger than the size of your tart pan. Carefully transfer the dough to the

prepared tart pan, pressing it gently into the bottom and sides of the pan. Trim any excess dough from the edges.

Prepare the Apple Filling:
- In a large mixing bowl, toss the thinly sliced apples with granulated sugar, ground cinnamon, lemon juice, and lemon zest until well coated.

Assemble the Tart:
- Arrange the apple slices in overlapping concentric circles over the prepared tart crust, starting from the outer edge and working your way towards the center.
- Brush the top of the apple slices with apricot jam or apple jelly to glaze.

Bake the Tart:
- Place the tart pan on a baking sheet to catch any drips, and bake in the preheated oven for 35-40 minutes, or until the crust is golden brown and the apples are tender.

Cool and Serve:
- Remove the tart from the oven and let it cool in the pan for about 10 minutes.
- Carefully remove the tart from the pan and transfer it to a wire rack to cool completely before slicing and serving.

Serve and Enjoy:
- Serve the Tarta de Manzana slices warm or at room temperature, optionally garnished with a dusting of powdered sugar or a dollop of whipped cream or vanilla ice cream.

This Tarta de Manzana is sure to impress with its buttery crust, tender apples, and aromatic cinnamon flavor—a perfect dessert to celebrate the flavors of Spain!

Turrones (Spanish Nougat)

Ingredients:

- 1 cup (240ml) honey
- 1 cup (200g) granulated sugar
- 2 large egg whites
- 2 cups (240g) toasted almonds (or other nuts of your choice), roughly chopped
- Edible rice paper (optional, for wrapping)

Instructions:

Prepare the Pan:
- Line a square or rectangular baking pan with parchment paper, leaving some overhang on the sides for easy removal later. Alternatively, you can use silicone molds for individual portions.

Prepare the Syrup:
- In a medium saucepan, combine the honey and granulated sugar. Heat over medium-low heat, stirring constantly, until the sugar is completely dissolved and the mixture reaches a temperature of 300°F (150°C) on a candy thermometer (hard-crack stage).

Whip the Egg Whites:
- While the syrup is cooking, in a separate mixing bowl, beat the egg whites until stiff peaks form.

Combine Syrup and Egg Whites:
- Once the syrup reaches the desired temperature, remove it from the heat and gradually pour it into the beaten egg whites, whisking continuously to incorporate.

Add Nuts:
- Fold the chopped toasted almonds (or other nuts) into the mixture until evenly distributed.

Shape and Set:
- Pour the mixture into the prepared baking pan or silicone molds, spreading it out evenly with a spatula.
- If desired, place a sheet of edible rice paper on top of the mixture to help with handling and prevent sticking.
- Allow the mixture to cool and set at room temperature for several hours, or preferably overnight.

Cut and Serve:

- Once the Turrones have set, use a sharp knife to cut them into desired shapes and sizes.
- Serve the Turrones as a delicious sweet treat or package them as homemade gifts for friends and family.

Turrones come in many variations, including hard and crunchy varieties (Turrón de Alicante), soft and chewy varieties (Turrón de Jijona), and those with additional ingredients like chocolate or dried fruits. Experiment with different nuts, flavorings, and textures to create your own unique Turrones at home!

Crema de Calabaza (Spanish Pumpkin Cream)

Ingredients:

- 1 medium-sized pumpkin (about 2-3 pounds), peeled, seeded, and diced
- 1 onion, chopped
- 2 cloves garlic, minced
- 4 cups (1 liter) vegetable or chicken broth
- 1 cup (240ml) heavy cream
- 2 tablespoons olive oil
- Salt and pepper to taste
- Optional garnishes: toasted pumpkin seeds, chopped fresh herbs (such as parsley or chives), a drizzle of olive oil, or a dollop of sour cream

Instructions:

Prepare the Pumpkin:
- Peel the pumpkin and remove the seeds. Cut the pumpkin into small cubes.

Sauté Onion and Garlic:
- In a large pot or Dutch oven, heat the olive oil over medium heat. Add the chopped onion and minced garlic, and sauté until softened and fragrant, about 5 minutes.

Cook the Pumpkin:
- Add the diced pumpkin to the pot, and season with salt and pepper to taste. Cook for another 5 minutes, stirring occasionally.

Add Broth:
- Pour in the vegetable or chicken broth, making sure the pumpkin is fully submerged. Bring the mixture to a boil, then reduce the heat to low and let it simmer for about 20-25 minutes, or until the pumpkin is tender and easily pierced with a fork.

Blend the Soup:
- Once the pumpkin is cooked, use an immersion blender or transfer the mixture to a blender in batches, and blend until smooth and creamy.

Add Cream:
- Return the blended soup to the pot (if necessary), and stir in the heavy cream. Heat the soup gently over low heat until warmed through, but do not boil.

Adjust Seasoning and Serve:
- Taste the soup and adjust the seasoning with salt and pepper as needed.
- Ladle the Crema de Calabaza into serving bowls, and garnish with toasted pumpkin seeds, chopped fresh herbs, a drizzle of olive oil, or a dollop of sour cream, if desired.

Serve and Enjoy:
- Serve the Crema de Calabaza hot as a comforting and nourishing soup, alongside crusty bread or your favorite salad.

This Crema de Calabaza is sure to warm you up on a chilly day with its velvety texture and delicious pumpkin flavor. It's a perfect dish to enjoy during the fall and winter seasons!

Yemas de Santa Teresa (Spanish Egg Yolk Candies)

Ingredients:

- 12 large egg yolks
- 1 cup (200g) granulated sugar
- 1/4 cup (60ml) water
- Confectioners' sugar, for dusting

Instructions:

Prepare the Egg Yolks:
- Separate the egg yolks from the egg whites, making sure to keep the yolks intact. Reserve the egg whites for another use.

Cook the Sugar Syrup:
- In a small saucepan, combine the granulated sugar and water. Heat the mixture over medium heat, stirring constantly, until the sugar is completely dissolved and the syrup reaches a temperature of 220°F (104°C) on a candy thermometer (soft-ball stage).

Prepare the Egg Yolk Mixture:
- In a large mixing bowl, lightly beat the egg yolks with a fork or whisk.
- Slowly pour the hot sugar syrup into the beaten egg yolks, whisking continuously to prevent the eggs from curdling.

Cook the Mixture:
- Transfer the egg yolk mixture back to the saucepan and place it over low heat. Cook the mixture gently, stirring constantly with a wooden spoon or silicone spatula, until it thickens and reaches a custard-like consistency. This should take about 5-7 minutes. Be careful not to overcook the mixture, as it can curdle or become grainy.

Cool the Mixture:
- Once the mixture has thickened, remove it from the heat and let it cool to room temperature. It will continue to thicken as it cools.

Shape the Yemas:
- Once the mixture has cooled, use a small spoon or melon baller to scoop out small portions of the mixture and roll them into smooth balls or oval shapes between your palms.

Dust with Confectioners' Sugar:
- Place the shaped Yemas de Santa Teresa on a tray lined with parchment paper, and dust them lightly with confectioners' sugar to prevent sticking.

Serve and Enjoy:
- Serve the Yemas de Santa Teresa as a delightful sweet treat, and enjoy their smooth and creamy texture and rich flavor.

These Yemas de Santa Teresa are sure to impress with their simplicity and decadence, making them a perfect addition to any dessert spread or festive occasion!

Borrachuelos (Spanish Anise Cookies)

Ingredients:

For the Dough:

- 3 cups (375g) all-purpose flour
- 1/2 cup (100g) granulated sugar
- 1/2 cup (120ml) dry white wine or anise liqueur (such as Anisette)
- 1/4 cup (60ml) olive oil or vegetable oil
- 1 teaspoon baking powder
- 1/2 teaspoon ground cinnamon
- Pinch of salt

For the Filling:

- 1 cup (200g) ground almonds
- 1/2 cup (100g) granulated sugar
- Zest of 1 lemon
- 1 teaspoon ground cinnamon
- 1/4 cup (60ml) dry white wine or anise liqueur (such as Anisette)

For Frying:

- Vegetable oil, for frying

For Dusting:

- Powdered sugar

Instructions:

Prepare the Dough:
- In a large mixing bowl, combine the all-purpose flour, granulated sugar, baking powder, ground cinnamon, and a pinch of salt.
- Gradually add the dry white wine (or anise liqueur) and olive oil, mixing until a smooth dough forms. Knead the dough for a few minutes until it

becomes elastic. If the dough is too dry, you can add a little more wine or oil as needed.
- Cover the dough with plastic wrap and let it rest for about 30 minutes.

Prepare the Filling:
- In a separate mixing bowl, combine the ground almonds, granulated sugar, lemon zest, ground cinnamon, and dry white wine (or anise liqueur). Mix until well combined to form a thick paste.

Assemble the Borrachuelos:
- Divide the dough into small portions and roll each portion into a ball.
- Flatten each ball into a thin circle or oval shape, about 1/8 inch (3mm) thick.
- Place a spoonful of the almond filling in the center of each dough circle.
- Fold the dough over the filling to enclose it completely, pressing the edges firmly to seal. You can shape them into rectangles, triangles, or half-moons, depending on your preference.

Fry the Borrachuelos:
- In a deep frying pan or pot, heat vegetable oil over medium heat until it reaches about 350°F (175°C).
- Carefully add the filled Borrachuelos to the hot oil, a few at a time, and fry them until golden brown and crispy on both sides, about 2-3 minutes per side.
- Remove the fried Borrachuelos from the oil using a slotted spoon and drain them on paper towels to remove excess oil.

Dust with Powdered Sugar:
- Once the Borrachuelos have cooled slightly, dust them generously with powdered sugar while still warm.

Serve and Enjoy:
- Serve the Borrachuelos as a delicious sweet treat, and enjoy their crispy exterior and flavorful almond filling.

These Borrachuelos are sure to be a hit with their unique flavor and delightful texture, making them a perfect addition to your holiday dessert table or any special occasion!

Bizcocho de Chocolate (Spanish Chocolate Cake)

Ingredients:

- 1 3/4 cups (220g) all-purpose flour
- 3/4 cup (65g) unsweetened cocoa powder
- 1 1/2 teaspoons baking powder
- 1 teaspoon baking soda
- 1/2 teaspoon salt
- 1 cup (200g) granulated sugar
- 3/4 cup (150g) packed light brown sugar
- 2 large eggs, at room temperature
- 1 cup (240ml) buttermilk, at room temperature
- 1/2 cup (120ml) vegetable oil
- 2 teaspoons vanilla extract
- 1 cup (240ml) hot water or brewed coffee

For the Chocolate Ganache:

- 1 cup (240ml) heavy cream
- 8 ounces (225g) semisweet or bittersweet chocolate, finely chopped
- 1 tablespoon unsalted butter, at room temperature

Instructions:

Preheat the Oven:
- Preheat your oven to 350°F (175°C). Grease and flour a 9-inch (23cm) round cake pan or line it with parchment paper.

Prepare the Dry Ingredients:
- In a large mixing bowl, sift together the all-purpose flour, cocoa powder, baking powder, baking soda, and salt. Whisk in the granulated sugar and light brown sugar until well combined.

Mix the Wet Ingredients:
- In another mixing bowl, whisk together the eggs, buttermilk, vegetable oil, and vanilla extract until smooth.

Combine Wet and Dry Ingredients:
- Gradually add the wet ingredients to the dry ingredients, mixing until just combined. Do not overmix.

- Stir in the hot water or brewed coffee until the batter is smooth. The batter will be thin, but that's okay.

Bake the Cake:
- Pour the batter into the prepared cake pan and smooth the top with a spatula.
- Bake in the preheated oven for 30-35 minutes, or until a toothpick inserted into the center of the cake comes out clean.
- Remove the cake from the oven and let it cool in the pan for about 10 minutes before transferring it to a wire rack to cool completely.

Make the Chocolate Ganache:
- In a small saucepan, heat the heavy cream over medium heat until it just begins to simmer. Remove from heat.
- Place the finely chopped chocolate in a heatproof bowl. Pour the hot cream over the chocolate and let it sit for 1-2 minutes.
- Add the butter to the bowl and whisk the mixture until smooth and glossy.

Assemble the Cake:
- Once the cake has cooled completely, pour the chocolate ganache over the top of the cake, allowing it to drip down the sides.
- Let the ganache set for about 15-20 minutes before slicing and serving.

Serve and Enjoy:
- Slice the Bizcocho de Chocolate and serve it as a decadent dessert, accompanied by whipped cream, vanilla ice cream, or fresh berries if desired.

This Bizcocho de Chocolate is sure to impress with its rich flavor and moist texture—a perfect indulgence for any chocolate lover!

Sopa de Fresas (Spanish Strawberry Soup)

Ingredients:

- 1 pound (450g) fresh strawberries, hulled and sliced
- 1/4 cup (50g) granulated sugar, or to taste
- 1 tablespoon fresh lemon juice
- 1/2 cup (120ml) cold water
- 1/2 cup (120ml) cold orange juice
- 1/4 cup (60ml) cold white wine (optional)
- Fresh mint leaves, for garnish
- Whipped cream or Greek yogurt, for serving (optional)

Instructions:

Prepare the Strawberries:
- Wash the strawberries under cold water and remove the stems. Slice the strawberries into quarters or halves, depending on their size.

Blend the Ingredients:
- In a blender or food processor, combine the sliced strawberries, granulated sugar, fresh lemon juice, cold water, cold orange juice, and cold white wine (if using). Blend until smooth and well combined. You can adjust the amount of sugar based on your preference and the sweetness of the strawberries.

Chill the Soup:
- Transfer the blended mixture to a large bowl or pitcher. Cover and refrigerate the soup for at least 1-2 hours, or until well chilled.

Serve:
- Once chilled, give the soup a stir to ensure it's well mixed. Taste and adjust the sweetness or tartness if necessary by adding more sugar or lemon juice.
- Ladle the Sopa de Fresas into serving bowls or glasses.
- Garnish each serving with fresh mint leaves for a pop of color and flavor.
- Serve the strawberry soup chilled, optionally accompanied by a dollop of whipped cream or a spoonful of Greek yogurt on top.

Enjoy:
- Serve the Sopa de Fresas as a refreshing dessert or sweet treat, perfect for cooling down on a warm day.

This Sopa de Fresas is bursting with the natural sweetness of ripe strawberries and the tangy freshness of citrus, making it a delightful and light dessert option for any occasion. Enjoy its vibrant flavors and cooling properties during the spring and summer months!

Crema de Chocolate (Spanish Chocolate Cream)

Ingredients:

- 2 cups (480ml) heavy cream
- 8 ounces (225g) semisweet or bittersweet chocolate, chopped
- 1/4 cup (50g) granulated sugar, or to taste
- 1 teaspoon vanilla extract
- Pinch of salt
- Optional toppings: whipped cream, chocolate shavings, or fresh berries

Instructions:

Heat the Cream:
- In a medium saucepan, heat the heavy cream over medium heat until it just begins to simmer. Do not let it come to a boil.

Melt the Chocolate:
- Place the chopped chocolate in a heatproof bowl. Pour the hot cream over the chocolate and let it sit for 1-2 minutes to soften the chocolate.
- Stir the mixture gently with a spatula until the chocolate is completely melted and the mixture is smooth and creamy.

Sweeten and Flavor:
- Stir in the granulated sugar, vanilla extract, and a pinch of salt, adjusting the sweetness to your taste preference. Keep in mind that the sweetness of the chocolate will also contribute to the overall sweetness of the dessert.

Chill the Chocolate Cream:
- Pour the chocolate cream mixture into individual serving dishes or a large bowl.
- Cover the dishes or bowl with plastic wrap, pressing the wrap directly onto the surface of the chocolate cream to prevent a skin from forming.
- Refrigerate the chocolate cream for at least 2-3 hours, or until well chilled and set.

Serve:
- Once chilled, remove the chocolate cream from the refrigerator.
- If desired, top each serving with a dollop of whipped cream, chocolate shavings, or fresh berries for garnish.

- Serve the Crema de Chocolate cold as a decadent dessert, perfect for any occasion.

Enjoy:
- Indulge in the creamy richness of the Crema de Chocolate, savoring each spoonful of velvety smoothness and intense chocolate flavor.

This Crema de Chocolate is sure to satisfy your chocolate cravings with its luxurious texture and irresistible taste. Enjoy it as a standalone dessert or use it as a filling for cakes, pastries, or tarts to elevate your sweet creations!

Torta de Santiago (Spanish Almond Cake)

Ingredients:

- 1 1/2 cups (180g) almond flour or finely ground almonds
- 1 cup (200g) granulated sugar
- 4 large eggs, separated
- Zest of 1 lemon
- Zest of 1 orange
- 1/4 cup (60ml) sweet wine or brandy (such as Moscatel or Amaretto)
- Confectioners' sugar, for dusting

Instructions:

Preheat the Oven:
- Preheat your oven to 350°F (175°C). Grease and flour a 9-inch (23cm) round cake pan.

Prepare the Batter:
- In a large mixing bowl, combine the almond flour and granulated sugar. Add the egg yolks, lemon zest, orange zest, and sweet wine or brandy. Mix until well combined and smooth.

Whip the Egg Whites:
- In a separate clean mixing bowl, beat the egg whites with a hand mixer or stand mixer until stiff peaks form.

Fold in Egg Whites:
- Gently fold the beaten egg whites into the almond mixture in two or three additions until evenly incorporated. Be careful not to deflate the egg whites too much.

Bake the Cake:
- Pour the batter into the prepared cake pan and spread it out evenly.
- Bake in the preheated oven for 30-35 minutes, or until the top is golden brown and a toothpick inserted into the center comes out clean.

Cool and Dust with Sugar:
- Remove the cake from the oven and let it cool in the pan for about 10 minutes. Then, carefully transfer it to a wire rack to cool completely.
- Once the cake has cooled, place a stencil of the cross of Saint James on top of the cake (optional), and dust the cake with confectioners' sugar. The cross can be made from paper or purchased as a stencil.

Serve:

- Slice the Torta de Santiago and serve it as a delightful dessert or snack, accompanied by a cup of coffee, tea, or a glass of sweet wine.

Enjoy:
- Enjoy the rich almond flavor and moist texture of the Torta de Santiago, a classic Spanish dessert that's perfect for any occasion.

This Torta de Santiago is not only delicious but also gluten-free, making it suitable for those with gluten sensitivities. Its simplicity and elegance make it a timeless dessert that's sure to impress!

Sobao Pasiego (Spanish Sponge Cake)

Ingredients:

- 1 cup (225g) unsalted butter, softened
- 1 cup (200g) granulated sugar
- 4 large eggs
- 1 teaspoon vanilla extract
- Zest of 1 lemon
- 2 cups (250g) all-purpose flour
- 1 1/2 teaspoons baking powder
- Pinch of salt
- Confectioners' sugar, for dusting (optional)

Instructions:

Preheat the Oven:
- Preheat your oven to 350°F (175°C). Grease and flour a 9-inch (23cm) square or round cake pan.

Cream the Butter and Sugar:
- In a large mixing bowl, cream together the softened unsalted butter and granulated sugar until light and fluffy.

Add Eggs and Flavorings:
- Add the eggs to the butter-sugar mixture one at a time, beating well after each addition. Stir in the vanilla extract and lemon zest until well combined.

Combine Dry Ingredients:
- In a separate mixing bowl, sift together the all-purpose flour, baking powder, and a pinch of salt.

Mix Batter:
- Gradually add the dry ingredients to the wet ingredients, mixing until just combined. Be careful not to overmix, as this can result in a tough cake.

Bake the Cake:
- Pour the batter into the prepared cake pan and spread it out evenly.
- Bake in the preheated oven for 30-35 minutes, or until the top is golden brown and a toothpick inserted into the center comes out clean.

Cool and Dust with Sugar:
- Remove the cake from the oven and let it cool in the pan for about 10 minutes. Then, carefully transfer it to a wire rack to cool completely.

- Once the cake has cooled, you can dust it with confectioners' sugar for a decorative touch, if desired.

Slice and Serve:
- Slice the Sobao Pasiego into squares or wedges and serve it as a delicious snack or dessert.
- Enjoy the buttery richness and delicate crumb of this traditional Spanish sponge cake.

This Sobao Pasiego is a classic treat that's perfect for enjoying with a cup of coffee or tea, or as a sweet ending to any meal. Its simplicity and irresistible flavor make it a beloved dessert in Spanish cuisine.

Buñuelos de Calabaza (Spanish Pumpkin Fritters)

Ingredients:

- 1 cup (200g) pumpkin puree (homemade or canned)
- 1 cup (125g) all-purpose flour
- 2 tablespoons granulated sugar
- 1 teaspoon baking powder
- 1/2 teaspoon ground cinnamon
- 1/4 teaspoon ground nutmeg
- Pinch of salt
- 1 large egg
- 1/4 cup (60ml) milk
- Vegetable oil, for frying
- Confectioners' sugar, for dusting

Instructions:

Prepare the Pumpkin Puree:
- If using fresh pumpkin, peel and dice the pumpkin into small pieces. Steam or boil the pumpkin until tender, then mash or puree it until smooth. If using canned pumpkin puree, skip this step.

Make the Batter:
- In a large mixing bowl, combine the pumpkin puree, all-purpose flour, granulated sugar, baking powder, ground cinnamon, ground nutmeg, and a pinch of salt. Mix until well combined.

Add the Egg and Milk:
- Beat the egg lightly in a small bowl, then add it to the pumpkin mixture along with the milk. Stir until a smooth batter forms. The consistency should be similar to pancake batter, thick but pourable. If the batter is too thick, you can add a little more milk.

Heat the Oil:
- In a deep frying pan or pot, heat vegetable oil to 350°F (175°C) over medium heat. The oil should be deep enough to fully submerge the fritters.

Fry the Fritters:
- Once the oil is hot, carefully drop spoonfuls of the batter into the oil using a tablespoon or small ice cream scoop. Make sure not to overcrowd the pan.

- Fry the fritters for 2-3 minutes on each side, or until they are golden brown and crispy. Use a slotted spoon to remove the fritters from the oil and transfer them to a plate lined with paper towels to drain any excess oil.

Dust with Confectioners' Sugar:
- While still warm, dust the Buñuelos de Calabaza generously with confectioners' sugar.

Serve Warm:
- Serve the pumpkin fritters warm as a delicious snack or dessert. They are best enjoyed fresh and crispy.

Enjoy:
- Indulge in the warm and comforting flavors of these Buñuelos de Calabaza, perfect for cozying up on a chilly day or celebrating the autumn season.

These Buñuelos de Calabaza are sure to be a hit with their irresistible pumpkin flavor and crispy exterior. Enjoy them with a cup of hot chocolate or your favorite warm beverage for a delightful treat!

Gachas Manchegas (Spanish Porridge)

Ingredients:

- 1 cup (125g) all-purpose flour
- 4 cups (960ml) water
- 4 tablespoons olive oil
- 2 cloves garlic, minced
- 1 teaspoon sweet paprika
- Salt, to taste

Instructions:

Prepare the Flour Mixture:
- In a small bowl, mix the all-purpose flour with 1 cup of water until smooth and well combined, ensuring there are no lumps.

Cook the Flour Mixture:
- In a large saucepan or pot, heat the olive oil over medium heat. Add the minced garlic and cook until fragrant, about 1-2 minutes.
- Gradually pour the flour mixture into the saucepan while stirring continuously to prevent lumps from forming.

Add Water:
- Once all the flour mixture has been added, gradually pour in the remaining 3 cups of water, stirring constantly to combine.

Season:
- Stir in the sweet paprika and season with salt to taste. Adjust the seasoning according to your preference.

Cook the Porridge:
- Bring the mixture to a gentle boil, then reduce the heat to low. Simmer the porridge, stirring occasionally, for about 15-20 minutes or until it thickens to a creamy consistency. The porridge should have a smooth texture.

Serve:
- Once the Gachas Manchegas are cooked to your desired consistency, remove the saucepan from the heat.
- Serve the porridge warm in individual bowls.

Garnish (Optional):
- You can garnish the Gachas Manchegas with additional olive oil drizzled on top before serving.

Enjoy:
- Enjoy the Gachas Manchegas as a comforting and satisfying dish, perfect for breakfast, brunch, or as a hearty snack.

Gachas Manchegas is a versatile dish that can be enjoyed on its own or accompanied by crusty bread, cheese, or cured meats. Its simple yet flavorful ingredients make it a staple in Spanish cuisine, particularly in the rural regions of La Mancha.

Pan de Higo (Spanish Fig Bread)

Ingredients:

- 2 cups (about 300g) dried figs, stemmed
- 1 cup (about 150g) dried dates, pitted
- 1 cup (about 150g) almonds, blanched and toasted
- 1/2 cup (about 75g) walnuts, toasted
- 1/2 cup (about 75g) hazelnuts, toasted
- 1/4 cup (about 30g) pine nuts, toasted
- Zest of 1 orange
- Zest of 1 lemon
- 1 teaspoon ground cinnamon
- 1/2 teaspoon ground cloves
- 1/4 teaspoon ground nutmeg
- 1/4 teaspoon ground anise (optional)
- 2-3 tablespoons brandy or rum (optional)
- Additional whole almonds or walnuts for decoration (optional)

Instructions:

Prepare the Ingredients:
- If the dried figs have stems, remove them. Also, make sure the dates are pitted.
- Blanch the almonds to remove the skins by placing them in boiling water for about 1 minute, then transferring them to a bowl of ice water. Once cooled, the skins should easily slip off. Toast the blanched almonds, walnuts, hazelnuts, and pine nuts in a dry skillet over medium heat until fragrant and lightly browned. Let them cool completely.

Chop the Fruits and Nuts:
- In a food processor, combine the dried figs, dates, toasted almonds, walnuts, hazelnuts, and pine nuts. Pulse the mixture until finely chopped and well combined. You can also chop the ingredients by hand if you prefer a coarser texture.

Add Flavorings:
- Add the orange zest, lemon zest, ground cinnamon, ground cloves, ground nutmeg, and ground anise (if using) to the mixture. Pulse or mix until the spices and zest are evenly distributed.

Optional: Add Brandy or Rum:
- For added flavor, you can add a couple of tablespoons of brandy or rum to the mixture. This is optional but adds a delicious depth of flavor.

Shape the Fig Bread:
- Transfer the mixture to a piece of parchment paper or plastic wrap. Shape it into a log or rectangular block, compacting it tightly with your hands to remove any air pockets. You can use the parchment paper or plastic wrap to help you shape and roll the mixture.

Decorate (Optional):
- If desired, press whole almonds or walnuts into the surface of the fig bread for decoration.

Chill and Serve:
- Wrap the shaped Pan de Higo tightly in plastic wrap or parchment paper and refrigerate for at least a few hours, or preferably overnight. Chilling helps the flavors meld together and makes the fig bread easier to slice.
- To serve, unwrap the Pan de Higo and slice it into rounds or bars.

Enjoy:
- Enjoy the Pan de Higo slices as a sweet and nutritious snack, dessert, or accompaniment to cheese and wine.

Pan de Higo is a delightful treat with a rich and earthy flavor from the dried fruits and nuts, complemented by the warm spices and citrus zest. It's perfect for enjoying during special occasions or as a wholesome snack any time of the day.

Ensaimadas (Spanish Sweet Rolls)

Ingredients:

- 4 cups (500g) bread flour
- 1/2 cup (100g) granulated sugar
- 2 teaspoons active dry yeast
- 3/4 cup (180ml) warm milk
- 1/2 cup (120ml) warm water
- 2 large eggs
- Zest of 1 lemon
- Zest of 1 orange
- 1/2 teaspoon salt
- 1/2 cup (115g) unsalted butter, softened
- Vegetable oil or lard, for greasing
- Powdered sugar, for dusting

Instructions:

Activate the Yeast:
- In a small bowl, dissolve 1 teaspoon of the granulated sugar in the warm milk. Sprinkle the active dry yeast over the milk and let it sit for about 5-10 minutes, or until frothy.

Prepare the Dough:
- In a large mixing bowl, combine the bread flour, remaining granulated sugar, lemon zest, orange zest, and salt. Make a well in the center of the dry ingredients.
- Pour the yeast mixture, warm water, and eggs into the well. Mix the ingredients together using a wooden spoon or your hands until a rough dough forms.

Knead the Dough:
- Transfer the dough to a lightly floured surface and knead it for about 10-12 minutes, or until it becomes smooth, elastic, and no longer sticky.
- Incorporate the softened unsalted butter into the dough, a little at a time, kneading until it is fully incorporated and the dough is smooth and shiny.

Let the Dough Rise:

- Place the dough in a lightly greased bowl, cover it with a clean kitchen towel or plastic wrap, and let it rise in a warm, draft-free place for about 1-2 hours, or until it has doubled in size.

Shape the Ensaimadas:
- Punch down the risen dough to deflate it, then divide it into equal portions. Roll each portion into a long rope, about 12 inches (30cm) in length.
- Take one end of the rope and coil it into a spiral shape, tucking the end underneath the coil. Repeat with the remaining dough portions.

Let the Ensaimadas Rise Again:
- Place the shaped Ensaimadas on a baking sheet lined with parchment paper, leaving some space between them to expand. Cover them loosely with a clean kitchen towel and let them rise for another 1-2 hours, or until puffy and almost doubled in size.

Bake the Ensaimadas:
- Preheat your oven to 350°F (175°C). Bake the risen Ensaimadas in the preheated oven for 15-20 minutes, or until golden brown and cooked through.
- Remove the Ensaimadas from the oven and let them cool on a wire rack for a few minutes before serving.

Dust with Powdered Sugar:
- Once cooled slightly, dust the Ensaimadas generously with powdered sugar before serving.

Enjoy:
- Serve the Ensaimadas warm or at room temperature as a delicious breakfast pastry or sweet treat.

These Ensaimadas are a delightful combination of soft, fluffy dough and subtle citrus flavor, making them a beloved pastry in Spanish cuisine. Enjoy them with a cup of coffee or hot chocolate for a truly indulgent experience!

Cabello de Ángel (Angel Hair Candy)

Ingredients:

- 1 small pumpkin (approximately 2-3 pounds)
- Granulated sugar
- Lemon zest (optional)
- Cinnamon stick (optional)

Instructions:

Prepare the Pumpkin:
- Start by washing the pumpkin thoroughly and cutting it into quarters. Remove the seeds and fibrous pulp from the center.

Cook the Pumpkin:
- Place the pumpkin quarters in a large pot and cover them with water. Bring the water to a boil over medium-high heat.
- Reduce the heat to low and simmer the pumpkin for about 30-40 minutes, or until it is soft and tender when pierced with a fork.

Drain and Mash the Pumpkin:
- Once the pumpkin is cooked, remove it from the pot and let it cool slightly. Use a spoon to scrape the flesh away from the skin.
- Mash the cooked pumpkin flesh with a fork or potato masher until it is smooth and free of lumps.

Extract the Strands:
- Take a handful of the mashed pumpkin and press it through a fine mesh sieve or colander with small holes. Use the back of a spoon to push the pumpkin through the holes.
- As you press the pumpkin through the sieve, thin strands of the pumpkin flesh will emerge on the other side, resembling "angel hair."

Sweeten the Strands:
- Transfer the strands of pumpkin to a clean pot or saucepan. Add granulated sugar to sweeten the pumpkin to your desired taste. The amount of sugar will depend on the sweetness of the pumpkin and your personal preference.
- Optionally, you can add lemon zest or a cinnamon stick to the pot for additional flavor.

Cook the Mixture:

- Place the pot over medium heat and cook the pumpkin strands with the sugar, stirring constantly, until the mixture thickens slightly and the sugar has dissolved completely. This usually takes about 10-15 minutes.

Cool and Store:
- Once cooked, remove the pot from the heat and let the Cabello de Ángel cool to room temperature.
- Transfer the Angel Hair Candy to a clean, airtight container and store it in the refrigerator until ready to use.

Serve:
- Use the Cabello de Ángel as a filling for pastries, cakes, or tarts. It's also delicious on its own as a sweet snack.

Cabello de Ángel adds a delicate sweetness and unique texture to desserts, making it a cherished ingredient in Spanish cuisine. Enjoy its ethereal strands in a variety of sweet creations!

Huesos de Santo (Spanish Saints' Bones)

Ingredients:

For the Marzipan Dough:

- 2 cups (250g) almond flour or finely ground almonds
- 1 1/4 cups (150g) powdered sugar
- 1-2 tablespoons water or lemon juice
- 1 teaspoon almond extract (optional)

For the Filling:

- Custard, chocolate ganache, fruit preserves, or any desired filling

For the Decoration:

- Powdered sugar or syrup glaze (optional)

Instructions:

    Prepare the Marzipan Dough:
- In a large mixing bowl, combine the almond flour and powdered sugar. If using almond extract, add it to the mixture.
- Gradually add water or lemon juice, one tablespoon at a time, while mixing, until the dough comes together. The dough should be pliable but not too sticky. Adjust the amount of liquid as needed.
- Knead the dough for a few minutes until smooth and uniform. If the dough is too dry, add a little more water or lemon juice.

    Shape the Marzipan:
- Divide the marzipan dough into small portions, each about the size of a walnut.
- Flatten each portion of dough into a thin, rectangular shape using your fingers or a rolling pin. The rectangles should be about 3-4 inches long and 1 inch wide.

    Add the Filling:

- Place a small amount of your desired filling along the center of each marzipan rectangle. Traditionally, custard or fruit preserves are common fillings for Huesos de Santo.
- Carefully roll the marzipan around the filling to form tube-shaped pastries. Seal the edges by pinching them together, ensuring the filling is completely enclosed.

Shape the Huesos de Santo:
- Using a knife, gently score the surface of each marzipan tube to create a bone-like texture, making diagonal lines across the surface.
- Alternatively, you can use the back of a fork to create indentations resembling bone markings.

Decoration (Optional):
- Dust the Huesos de Santo with powdered sugar for a simple and traditional decoration. Alternatively, you can glaze them with a syrup made from sugar and water, flavored with lemon or orange zest.

Serve:
- Allow the Huesos de Santo to set for a while before serving, allowing the filling to firm up slightly.
- Serve the pastries as a delicious and festive dessert for All Saints' Day or any special occasion.

Huesos de Santo are not only visually striking but also deliciously sweet, making them a beloved treat in Spanish cuisine, particularly during the autumn season. Enjoy these delightful pastries as a delightful homage to Spanish culinary traditions!

Crema de Orujo (Spanish Cream Liqueur)

Ingredients:

- 1 cup (240ml) orujo (Spanish grape pomace spirit) or grappa
- 1 cup (240ml) heavy cream
- 1/2 cup (100g) granulated sugar
- 1 teaspoon vanilla extract
- Optional flavorings: instant coffee powder, cocoa powder, orange zest, or other desired flavorings

Instructions:

Combine Ingredients:
- In a mixing bowl, combine the orujo (or grappa), heavy cream, granulated sugar, and vanilla extract. Stir until the sugar is completely dissolved and the ingredients are well combined.

Add Optional Flavorings:
- If desired, add flavorings such as instant coffee powder (for a coffee-flavored liqueur), cocoa powder (for a chocolate-flavored liqueur), orange zest (for a citrusy twist), or any other flavorings of your choice. Adjust the quantities to taste.

Mix Thoroughly:
- Mix the ingredients thoroughly to ensure that the flavorings are evenly distributed throughout the mixture.

Strain (Optional):
- If you prefer a smoother texture, you can strain the mixture through a fine-mesh sieve or cheesecloth to remove any solid particles or zest.

Bottle and Store:
- Transfer the Crema de Orujo to clean glass bottles or jars with tight-fitting lids.
- Seal the bottles tightly and store them in the refrigerator for at least a few hours, or preferably overnight, to chill and allow the flavors to meld together.

Serve:
- Serve the Crema de Orujo chilled as a delicious after-dinner digestif or dessert liqueur.

- Enjoy it neat in small glasses or over ice. You can also use it as a creamy and flavorful addition to coffee, hot chocolate, or cocktails.

Storage:
- Store any leftover Crema de Orujo in the refrigerator for up to a few weeks. Shake or stir before serving, as it may separate slightly over time.

Crema de Orujo is a delightful and versatile liqueur that's perfect for sipping on its own or incorporating into various cocktails and desserts. Enjoy its smooth texture and rich flavor as a luxurious treat!

Tarta de Melocotón (Spanish Peach Tart)

Ingredients:

For the Pastry Crust:

- 1 1/4 cups (150g) all-purpose flour
- 1/4 cup (50g) granulated sugar
- 1/2 cup (115g) unsalted butter, cold and cut into small pieces
- 1 large egg yolk
- 2-3 tablespoons cold water

For the Filling:

- 1/2 cup (100g) granulated sugar
- 1/4 cup (30g) all-purpose flour
- 1/2 teaspoon vanilla extract
- 2 large eggs
- 1/2 cup (120ml) heavy cream or milk
- 1/2 cup (120ml) almond milk or almond extract (optional)
- 3-4 ripe peaches, thinly sliced

For Glaze (optional):

- 2 tablespoons apricot preserves or peach jam
- 1 tablespoon water

Instructions:

Prepare the Pastry Crust:
- In a large mixing bowl, combine the all-purpose flour and granulated sugar. Add the cold, diced butter, and use your fingertips or a pastry cutter to rub or cut the butter into the flour mixture until it resembles coarse crumbs.
- Add the egg yolk and cold water, and mix until the dough comes together. If the dough is too dry, add more water, 1 tablespoon at a time.
- Shape the dough into a flat disk, wrap it in plastic wrap, and refrigerate for at least 30 minutes.

Preheat the Oven:
- Preheat your oven to 375°F (190°C). Grease a tart pan with removable bottom or a pie dish.

Roll Out the Dough:
- On a lightly floured surface, roll out the chilled pastry dough into a circle slightly larger than your tart pan or pie dish. Carefully transfer the rolled-out dough to the prepared pan and press it gently into the bottom and sides.

Prepare the Filling:
- In a mixing bowl, whisk together the granulated sugar, all-purpose flour, vanilla extract, eggs, heavy cream (or milk), and almond milk (or almond extract), if using, until smooth and well combined.

Assemble the Tart:
- Pour the filling mixture into the prepared pastry crust. Arrange the thinly sliced peaches on top of the filling in a decorative pattern.

Bake the Tart:
- Place the tart pan on a baking sheet and transfer it to the preheated oven. Bake for 30-35 minutes, or until the filling is set and the crust is golden brown.

Optional Glaze:
- In a small saucepan, heat the apricot preserves or peach jam with water over low heat until melted and smooth. Brush the glaze over the top of the warm tart for a glossy finish.

Cool and Serve:
- Allow the Tarta de Melocotón to cool in the pan for a few minutes before transferring it to a wire rack to cool completely.
- Serve the tart slices at room temperature, optionally accompanied by whipped cream or vanilla ice cream.

Enjoy:
- Enjoy the delicious Tarta de Melocotón, with its buttery crust, creamy filling, and fresh peach slices, as a delightful dessert for any occasion!

This Tarta de Melocotón is a wonderful way to celebrate the sweetness of ripe peaches in a classic Spanish-inspired dessert.

Polvorón de Canela (Spanish Cinnamon Shortbread)

Ingredients:

- 2 cups (250g) all-purpose flour
- 1 cup (225g) unsalted butter, softened
- 1 cup (120g) powdered sugar
- 1 teaspoon ground cinnamon
- 1/2 teaspoon vanilla extract
- Pinch of salt
- Additional powdered sugar for dusting

Instructions:

Preheat the Oven:
- Preheat your oven to 350°F (175°C). Line a baking sheet with parchment paper or a silicone baking mat.

Prepare the Dough:
- In a mixing bowl, cream together the softened unsalted butter and powdered sugar until light and fluffy.
- Add the vanilla extract and ground cinnamon to the butter mixture, and mix until well combined.

Incorporate the Flour:
- Gradually add the all-purpose flour and a pinch of salt to the butter mixture, mixing until a soft dough forms. Be careful not to overmix.

Shape the Cookies:
- Take tablespoonfuls of the dough and roll them into balls. Place the balls of dough onto the prepared baking sheet, spacing them a couple of inches apart.

Flatten the Cookies:
- Use the bottom of a glass or a cookie stamp to gently flatten each ball of dough into a round disc, about 1/2 inch thick.

Bake the Cookies:
- Place the baking sheet in the preheated oven and bake the cookies for 12-15 minutes, or until the edges are lightly golden brown.
- Remove the cookies from the oven and let them cool on the baking sheet for a few minutes before transferring them to a wire rack to cool completely.

Dust with Powdered Sugar:
- Once the cookies have cooled completely, dust them generously with powdered sugar. You can use a fine-mesh sieve to evenly coat the cookies with powdered sugar.

Serve and Enjoy:
- Serve the Polvorón de Canela cookies with a cup of coffee or tea for a delightful treat. Enjoy their buttery texture and delicate cinnamon flavor!

These Polvorón de Canela cookies are perfect for holiday gatherings, cookie exchanges, or simply as a sweet indulgence any time of the year. Their crumbly texture and warm cinnamon aroma make them a beloved treat in Spanish cuisine.

Tejas de Almendra (Almond Tile Cookies)

Ingredients:

- 1 cup (100g) almond flour or finely ground almonds
- 1/2 cup (100g) granulated sugar
- 1/4 cup (30g) all-purpose flour
- Pinch of salt
- 2 large egg whites
- 1/2 teaspoon almond extract
- 1/4 cup (55g) unsalted butter, melted
- Sliced almonds, for garnish (optional)

Instructions:

Preheat the Oven:
- Preheat your oven to 350°F (175°C). Line a baking sheet with parchment paper or a silicone baking mat.

Prepare the Batter:
- In a mixing bowl, combine the almond flour, granulated sugar, all-purpose flour, and a pinch of salt. Mix until well combined.
- In a separate bowl, whisk together the egg whites and almond extract until frothy.

Combine Wet and Dry Ingredients:
- Gradually add the frothy egg white mixture to the dry ingredients, stirring until a smooth batter forms.
- Pour in the melted unsalted butter and mix until everything is well combined and the batter is smooth.

Shape the Cookies:
- Drop teaspoonfuls of the batter onto the prepared baking sheet, spacing them a few inches apart. Use the back of a spoon to spread the batter into thin circles, resembling tiles.
- If desired, garnish each cookie with a few sliced almonds for added texture and decoration.

Bake the Cookies:
- Place the baking sheet in the preheated oven and bake the cookies for 8-10 minutes, or until the edges are golden brown and the cookies are firm to the touch.

- Keep a close eye on the cookies as they bake, as they can quickly go from golden brown to burnt.

Shape the Cookies:
- While the cookies are still warm and pliable, use a spatula or knife to gently lift them from the baking sheet and drape them over a rolling pin or the edge of a cup to create a curved shape, resembling tiles.
- Alternatively, you can leave the cookies flat if you prefer.

Cool and Serve:
- Allow the Tejas de Almendra cookies to cool completely on a wire rack before serving.
- Serve the cookies as a delightful sweet treat with a cup of coffee or tea, or package them in a decorative box to give as gifts.

These Tejas de Almendra cookies are wonderfully crisp and almond-flavored, making them a delightful addition to any dessert spread or cookie platter. Enjoy their delicate texture and nutty aroma!

Frutas de Aragón (Spanish Fruit Candies)

Ingredients:

- 1 cup fresh cherries or other small fruits (such as strawberries, apricots, or figs)
- 1 cup granulated sugar
- 1 cup water
- 8 ounces dark or milk chocolate, chopped

Instructions:

Prepare the Fruits:
- Wash the cherries or other small fruits thoroughly and remove any stems or leaves. If using larger fruits like strawberries, apricots, or figs, cut them into bite-sized pieces.

Make the Syrup:
- In a saucepan, combine the granulated sugar and water. Heat the mixture over medium heat, stirring occasionally, until the sugar is completely dissolved and the syrup comes to a gentle boil.

Candy the Fruits:
- Add the prepared fruits to the boiling syrup. Reduce the heat to low and simmer the fruits in the syrup for 10-15 minutes, or until they are slightly softened and translucent.
- Remove the saucepan from the heat and let the fruits cool in the syrup for about 30 minutes.

Drain the Fruits:
- Using a slotted spoon, carefully remove the candied fruits from the syrup and place them on a wire rack set over a baking sheet. Allow any excess syrup to drip off the fruits.

Cool and Dry:
- Let the candied fruits cool completely at room temperature for several hours or overnight. They should be slightly tacky to the touch but not overly sticky.

Coat with Chocolate:
- Once the candied fruits are dry, melt the chopped chocolate in a heatproof bowl set over a pot of simmering water (double boiler), stirring until smooth.

- Dip each candied fruit into the melted chocolate, using a fork or dipping tool to coat it completely. Tap off any excess chocolate and place the coated fruit back onto the wire rack.

Set the Chocolate:
- Allow the chocolate-coated fruits to set at room temperature or in the refrigerator until the chocolate hardens and forms a thin shell around the fruits.

Serve or Store:
- Once the chocolate is set, the Frutas de Aragón are ready to serve. Enjoy them as a delightful sweet treat or package them in decorative boxes to give as gifts.
- Store any leftover candies in an airtight container at room temperature for up to a week, or in the refrigerator for longer shelf life.

These homemade Frutas de Aragón are a delicious combination of sweet, tart, and chocolatey flavors, making them a delightful indulgence for any occasion. Enjoy the taste of Spain with these traditional fruit candies!

Crema de Limón (Spanish Lemon Cream)

Ingredients:

- 4 large lemons
- 1 cup (200g) granulated sugar
- 4 large eggs
- 1/2 cup (120ml) heavy cream
- Pinch of salt
- Zest of 1 lemon (optional, for garnish)

Instructions:

Prepare the Lemon Zest:
- Using a fine grater or zester, carefully zest the lemons to create thin strips of lemon peel. Set aside the zest for garnish, if desired.

Extract the Lemon Juice:
- Roll the lemons on a flat surface to soften them, then cut them in half and juice them using a citrus juicer or reamer. Strain the lemon juice through a fine-mesh sieve to remove any seeds or pulp.

Make the Lemon Cream:
- In a heatproof bowl, whisk together the granulated sugar, eggs, and lemon juice until well combined.
- Place the bowl over a pot of simmering water (double boiler) and cook the mixture, whisking constantly, until it thickens and coats the back of a spoon. This usually takes about 10-15 minutes.
- Remove the bowl from the heat and let the lemon cream cool slightly.

Add Heavy Cream:
- In a separate bowl, whip the heavy cream until soft peaks form.
- Gently fold the whipped cream into the cooled lemon cream mixture until smooth and well combined. The whipped cream will lighten the texture of the lemon cream and give it a mousse-like consistency.

Chill the Lemon Cream:
- Transfer the Crema de Limón to serving bowls or individual ramekins. Cover them with plastic wrap and refrigerate for at least 2-3 hours, or until the cream is chilled and set.

Garnish and Serve:
- Before serving, garnish the Crema de Limón with lemon zest, if desired.

- Serve the lemon cream chilled, either on its own or accompanied by fresh berries, mint leaves, or shortbread cookies for a delightful dessert.

Enjoy:
- Enjoy the refreshing and tangy flavor of Crema de Limón as a delicious ending to any meal or as a light and refreshing treat on a warm day.

This Crema de Limón recipe captures the essence of fresh lemons in a creamy and luscious dessert that's sure to brighten your day. Indulge in the zesty goodness of Spanish Lemon Cream!

Tocino de Cielo (Heaven's Bacon)

Ingredients:

- 12 egg yolks
- 1 cup (200g) granulated sugar
- 1/2 cup (120ml) water
- Caramel sauce (optional, for serving)

Instructions:

Preheat the Oven:
- Preheat your oven to 350°F (175°C). Place a baking dish filled with water on the bottom rack of the oven to create a water bath.

Prepare the Caramel:
- If you're using caramel sauce, prepare it by melting sugar in a saucepan over medium heat until it turns amber in color. Pour the caramel into the bottom of individual ramekins or a large baking dish, swirling to coat the bottoms evenly. Allow the caramel to cool and harden.

Make the Egg Yolk Mixture:
- In a large mixing bowl, whisk together the egg yolks and granulated sugar until well combined and slightly thickened.

Prepare the Syrup:
- In a separate saucepan, combine the water and sugar over medium heat. Stir until the sugar is completely dissolved, then remove from heat and let it cool slightly.

Combine the Mixtures:
- Gradually pour the warm sugar syrup into the egg yolk mixture, stirring constantly until smooth and well combined. The resulting mixture should be thin and pourable.

Strain the Mixture:
- Strain the egg yolk mixture through a fine-mesh sieve to remove any lumps or air bubbles.

Pour into Ramekins:
- Pour the strained egg yolk mixture into the prepared ramekins or baking dish with caramel sauce, filling them almost to the top.

Bake in Water Bath:

- Place the filled ramekins or baking dish in the preheated oven, inside the water bath, and bake for about 30-40 minutes, or until the Tocino de Cielo is set but still slightly jiggly in the center.

Cool and Chill:
- Remove the Tocino de Cielo from the oven and let it cool to room temperature. Then, refrigerate for at least 2-3 hours, or until fully chilled and set.

Serve:
- Once chilled, run a knife around the edges of the ramekins or dish to loosen the Tocino de Cielo. Carefully invert each serving onto a plate to unmold, allowing the caramel sauce to drizzle over the top.

Enjoy:
- Serve the Tocino de Cielo chilled as a luxurious and indulgent dessert, enjoying its creamy texture and rich flavor reminiscent of caramelized custard.

Tocino de Cielo is a heavenly dessert that's sure to impress with its silky smooth texture and delicate sweetness. Enjoy this Spanish delicacy as a delightful finale to any meal!

Goxua (Basque Trifle)

Ingredients:

For the Sponge Cake:

- 4 large eggs
- 1 cup (200g) granulated sugar
- 1 cup (125g) all-purpose flour
- 1 teaspoon baking powder
- Pinch of salt

For the Pastry Cream:

- 2 cups (480ml) whole milk
- 4 large egg yolks
- 1/2 cup (100g) granulated sugar
- 1/4 cup (30g) cornstarch
- 1 teaspoon vanilla extract

For Assembly:

- Caramelized sugar (made from 1 cup granulated sugar)
- Whipped cream (sweetened to taste)
- Cherries or berries for garnish (optional)

Instructions:

Prepare the Sponge Cake:
- Preheat your oven to 350°F (175°C). Grease and flour a 9x13-inch baking pan.
- In a large mixing bowl, beat the eggs and granulated sugar together until thick and pale.
- Sift the flour, baking powder, and salt together. Gradually fold the dry ingredients into the egg mixture until just combined.

- Pour the batter into the prepared baking pan and smooth the top. Bake for 20-25 minutes or until a toothpick inserted into the center comes out clean.
- Remove the sponge cake from the oven and let it cool completely in the pan.

Make the Pastry Cream:
- In a saucepan, heat the whole milk over medium heat until steaming but not boiling.
- In a separate bowl, whisk together the egg yolks, granulated sugar, and cornstarch until smooth and pale yellow.
- Gradually pour the hot milk into the egg yolk mixture, whisking constantly to temper the eggs.
- Return the mixture to the saucepan and cook over medium heat, stirring constantly, until thickened.
- Remove from heat and stir in the vanilla extract. Transfer the pastry cream to a bowl and cover with plastic wrap, pressing it directly onto the surface to prevent a skin from forming. Chill in the refrigerator until cold.

Assembly:
- Once the sponge cake and pastry cream are cooled, cut the sponge cake into squares or rectangles to fit the serving glasses or bowls.
- Place a layer of sponge cake at the bottom of each serving vessel. Drizzle with caramelized sugar.
- Spoon a layer of pastry cream over the sponge cake, spreading it out evenly.
- Top the pastry cream with another layer of sponge cake and drizzle with more caramelized sugar.
- Finish with a generous dollop of sweetened whipped cream on top.
- Garnish with cherries or berries if desired.

Chill and Serve:
- Refrigerate the Goxua for at least 1-2 hours before serving to allow the flavors to meld and the dessert to set.
- Serve chilled and enjoy the layers of flavor and texture in this delightful Basque trifle.

Goxua is a heavenly dessert that's sure to impress with its decadent layers of sponge cake, pastry cream, caramelized sugar, and whipped cream. Enjoy this traditional Basque treat as a delightful finale to any meal or special occasion!

Migas Extremeñas (Spanish Crumb Cake)

Ingredients:

- 2 cups (about 200g) stale bread crumbs
- 1 cup (about 100g) ground almonds
- 1 cup (200g) granulated sugar
- 1 teaspoon ground cinnamon
- 1/2 teaspoon ground cloves
- 1/2 teaspoon ground nutmeg
- Zest of 1 lemon
- Zest of 1 orange
- 4 large eggs, beaten
- 1/2 cup (120ml) olive oil
- 1/4 cup (60ml) sweet wine (such as Pedro Ximénez or Muscatel)
- Powdered sugar, for dusting (optional)

Instructions:

Preheat the Oven:
- Preheat your oven to 350°F (175°C). Grease a round cake pan or line it with parchment paper.

Prepare the Dry Ingredients:
- In a large mixing bowl, combine the stale bread crumbs, ground almonds, granulated sugar, ground cinnamon, ground cloves, ground nutmeg, lemon zest, and orange zest. Mix well to combine.

Add the Wet Ingredients:
- In a separate bowl, whisk together the beaten eggs, olive oil, and sweet wine until well combined.

Combine the Mixtures:
- Pour the wet ingredients into the bowl of dry ingredients. Use a spatula or wooden spoon to mix everything together until well combined and a thick batter forms.

Transfer to the Cake Pan:
- Pour the batter into the prepared cake pan, spreading it out evenly with a spatula.

Bake the Cake:

- Place the cake pan in the preheated oven and bake for 35-40 minutes, or until the cake is golden brown and a toothpick inserted into the center comes out clean.

Cool and Serve:
- Remove the cake from the oven and let it cool in the pan for 10-15 minutes. Then, carefully transfer it to a wire rack to cool completely.

Optional: Dust with Powdered Sugar:
- Once the cake has cooled, you can dust it with powdered sugar for a decorative touch, if desired.

Slice and Enjoy:
- Slice the Migas Extremeñas into wedges and serve at room temperature as a delightful dessert or snack.

Migas Extremeñas is a unique and flavorful cake that showcases the rustic charm of Spanish cuisine. Enjoy its rich texture and aromatic spices with a cup of coffee or tea for a delightful treat!

Hornazo (Spanish Easter Cake)

Ingredients:

For the Dough:

- 4 cups (500g) all-purpose flour
- 1 cup (240ml) warm water
- 1/4 cup (60ml) olive oil
- 1 teaspoon salt
- 1 packet (7g) active dry yeast
- 1 teaspoon sugar

For the Filling:

- 1/2 lb (225g) pork loin, cooked and diced
- 1/2 lb (225g) chorizo sausage, sliced
- 4 hard-boiled eggs, peeled and sliced
- Salt and pepper to taste
- Optional: sliced ham, bacon, or other cooked meats

For Glazing:

- 1 egg, beaten (for egg wash)

Instructions:

    Prepare the Dough:
- In a small bowl, combine the warm water, sugar, and yeast. Let it sit for about 5-10 minutes until foamy.
- In a large mixing bowl, combine the flour and salt. Make a well in the center and pour in the yeast mixture and olive oil.
- Stir until a dough forms, then knead the dough on a floured surface for about 5-7 minutes until smooth and elastic. Place the dough in a greased bowl, cover with a clean kitchen towel, and let it rise in a warm place for about 1-2 hours, or until doubled in size.

    Prepare the Filling:
- In a mixing bowl, combine the cooked diced pork loin, sliced chorizo, and any other cooked meats you're using. Season with salt and pepper to taste and mix well.

Assemble the Hornazo:
- Preheat your oven to 375°F (190°C). Grease a baking sheet or line it with parchment paper.
- Punch down the risen dough and divide it into two equal portions. Roll out each portion into a rectangle or oval shape, about 1/4 inch thick.
- Place one portion of the rolled-out dough onto the prepared baking sheet. Spread the filling mixture evenly over the dough, leaving a border around the edges. Arrange the sliced hard-boiled eggs over the filling.
- Place the second portion of rolled-out dough over the filling and crimp the edges to seal the pie. Brush the top with beaten egg for a golden finish.

Bake the Hornazo:
- Transfer the assembled Hornazo to the preheated oven and bake for 30-40 minutes, or until the crust is golden brown and the filling is cooked through.

Cool and Serve:
- Remove the Hornazo from the oven and let it cool slightly before slicing and serving. Serve warm or at room temperature as a delicious Easter treat.

Hornazo is a flavorful and satisfying dish that is perfect for celebrating Easter or any special occasion. Enjoy the combination of savory meats and tender dough in this traditional Spanish pastry!

Pastissets (Spanish Pastry)

Ingredients:

For the Dough:

- 2 cups (250g) all-purpose flour
- 1/2 cup (100g) granulated sugar
- 1/2 cup (115g) unsalted butter, softened
- 2 large eggs
- 1 teaspoon baking powder
- Zest of 1 lemon
- Pinch of salt

For the Filling:

- 1 cup (100g) ground almonds
- 1/2 cup (100g) granulated sugar
- 1 teaspoon ground cinnamon
- 1/4 teaspoon almond extract (optional)
- Jam of your choice (apricot, raspberry, or cherry work well)
- Vegetable oil, for frying
- Powdered sugar, for dusting

Instructions:

Prepare the Dough:
- In a mixing bowl, cream together the softened unsalted butter and granulated sugar until light and fluffy.
- Add the eggs, one at a time, beating well after each addition. Stir in the lemon zest.
- In a separate bowl, sift together the all-purpose flour, baking powder, and salt. Gradually add the dry ingredients to the wet ingredients, mixing until a soft dough forms. If the dough is too sticky, you can add a little more flour.

Make the Filling:

- In a bowl, combine the ground almonds, granulated sugar, ground cinnamon, and almond extract (if using). Mix until well combined to make the almond filling.

Shape the Pastissets:
- On a lightly floured surface, roll out the dough to a thickness of about 1/4 inch. Use a round cookie cutter or glass to cut out circles of dough.
- Place a small spoonful of the almond filling in the center of each dough circle. Top with a small dollop of jam.
- Fold the dough over the filling to create a half-moon shape, then use a fork to seal the edges.

Fry the Pastissets:
- In a deep skillet or frying pan, heat vegetable oil to 350°F (175°C).
- Carefully place the pastissets in the hot oil, a few at a time, and fry until golden brown on both sides, about 2-3 minutes per side.
- Use a slotted spoon to transfer the fried pastissets to a paper towel-lined plate to drain excess oil.

Serve and Enjoy:
- Once the pastissets have cooled slightly, dust them with powdered sugar.
- Serve the pastissets warm or at room temperature as a delightful sweet treat for any occasion.

These Pastissets are sure to be a hit with their crispy exterior, tender interior, and delicious almond and jam filling. Enjoy them with a cup of coffee or tea for a delightful snack or dessert.

Carajitos de Jerez (Spanish Almond Cookies)

Ingredients:

- 2 cups (200g) almond flour
- 1 cup (200g) granulated sugar
- 2 large egg whites
- 1/2 teaspoon almond extract
- Pinch of salt
- Powdered sugar, for dusting (optional)

Instructions:

Preheat the Oven:
- Preheat your oven to 350°F (175°C). Line a baking sheet with parchment paper or a silicone baking mat.

Mix the Ingredients:
- In a mixing bowl, combine the almond flour, granulated sugar, almond extract, and a pinch of salt. Mix until well combined.

Whip the Egg Whites:
- In a separate bowl, beat the egg whites until stiff peaks form.

Incorporate Egg Whites:
- Gently fold the whipped egg whites into the almond mixture until a thick dough forms. Be careful not to deflate the egg whites too much.

Shape the Cookies:
- Take tablespoonfuls of the dough and roll them into balls. Place the balls of dough onto the prepared baking sheet, spacing them a couple of inches apart.

Flatten the Cookies:
- Use the back of a fork to gently flatten each ball of dough, creating a crisscross pattern on top.

Bake the Cookies:
- Place the baking sheet in the preheated oven and bake the cookies for 10-12 minutes, or until they are lightly golden brown around the edges.

Cool and Dust with Powdered Sugar:
- Remove the cookies from the oven and let them cool on the baking sheet for a few minutes before transferring them to a wire rack to cool completely.

- Once cooled, dust the Carajitos de Jerez with powdered sugar, if desired, for a decorative touch.

Serve and Enjoy:
- Serve the Carajitos de Jerez with a cup of coffee or tea for a delightful treat. Enjoy the crunchy texture and rich almond flavor of these traditional Spanish cookies!

These Carajitos de Jerez are simple to make and are sure to be a hit with their delicious flavor and satisfying crunch. They are perfect for serving at parties, gatherings, or as a sweet indulgence any time of day.

Crema de Naranja (Spanish Orange Cream)

Ingredients:

- 2 cups (480ml) freshly squeezed orange juice
- Zest of 2 oranges
- 4 large eggs
- 1/2 cup (100g) granulated sugar
- 1/4 cup (30g) cornstarch
- 1 cup (240ml) heavy cream
- Fresh orange segments and mint leaves, for garnish (optional)

Instructions:

Prepare the Orange Juice:
- Squeeze the oranges to extract 2 cups of fresh orange juice. Strain the juice to remove any pulp or seeds.

Zest the Oranges:
- Use a fine grater or zester to remove the zest from two oranges. Set the zest aside for later use.

Make the Orange Custard:
- In a saucepan, whisk together the orange juice, orange zest, eggs, granulated sugar, and cornstarch until smooth.
- Place the saucepan over medium heat and cook the mixture, stirring constantly, until it thickens and comes to a gentle boil. This usually takes about 5-7 minutes.
- Once the mixture has thickened, remove it from the heat and let it cool slightly.

Prepare the Whipped Cream:
- In a separate bowl, whip the heavy cream until soft peaks form.

Combine the Mixtures:
- Gradually fold the whipped cream into the cooled orange custard mixture until smooth and well combined. The whipped cream will lighten the texture of the cream and give it a luxurious consistency.

Chill the Orange Cream:
- Transfer the Crema de Naranja to serving bowls or individual ramekins. Cover them with plastic wrap and refrigerate for at least 2-3 hours, or until the cream is chilled and set.

Garnish and Serve:
- Before serving, garnish the Crema de Naranja with fresh orange segments and mint leaves, if desired, for a pop of color and freshness.
- Serve the orange cream chilled, either on its own or accompanied by crisp almond cookies or shortbread biscuits for a delightful dessert.

Crema de Naranja is a light and creamy dessert that showcases the bright and sunny flavor of oranges. Enjoy its refreshing taste and smooth texture as a delightful ending to any meal!

Empanada Gallega (Galician Sweet Pie)

Ingredients:

For the Dough:

- 2 cups (250g) all-purpose flour
- 1/2 cup (100g) granulated sugar
- 1/2 cup (115g) unsalted butter, chilled and cubed
- 1 large egg
- Pinch of salt

For the Filling:

- 4-5 large apples, peeled, cored, and thinly sliced
- 1/2 cup (100g) granulated sugar
- 1 teaspoon ground cinnamon
- 1/4 teaspoon ground nutmeg
- 1/4 teaspoon ground cloves
- 1/2 cup (50g) ground almonds
- Zest of 1 lemon
- 1 tablespoon lemon juice
- 2 tablespoons unsalted butter, melted

For Glazing:

- 1 egg, beaten (for egg wash)
- Granulated sugar, for sprinkling

Instructions:

Prepare the Dough:
- In a large mixing bowl, combine the all-purpose flour, granulated sugar, and pinch of salt. Add the chilled cubed butter and rub it into the flour mixture until it resembles coarse crumbs.
- Beat the egg and add it to the mixture, stirring until a dough forms. If the dough is too dry, you can add a tablespoon of cold water at a time until it comes together.
- Shape the dough into a ball, wrap it in plastic wrap, and refrigerate it for at least 30 minutes.

Make the Filling:
- In a large bowl, toss the sliced apples with granulated sugar, ground cinnamon, ground nutmeg, ground cloves, ground almonds, lemon zest, and lemon juice until well combined.

Assemble the Empanada:
- Preheat your oven to 350°F (175°C). Grease a round baking pan or line it with parchment paper.
- On a lightly floured surface, roll out two-thirds of the chilled dough into a circle large enough to line the bottom and sides of the prepared baking pan. Transfer the dough to the pan and press it gently into the bottom and sides.
- Spread the prepared apple filling evenly over the dough in the pan. Drizzle the melted butter over the filling.

Add the Top Crust:
- Roll out the remaining one-third of the chilled dough into a circle large enough to cover the filling in the pan. Place the dough over the filling and press the edges to seal, crimping with a fork or your fingers. Trim any excess dough.

Glaze and Bake:
- Brush the top crust with beaten egg and sprinkle with granulated sugar for a golden finish.
- Use a sharp knife to make a few small slits in the top crust to allow steam to escape during baking.
- Bake the Empanada Gallega in the preheated oven for 40-45 minutes, or until the crust is golden brown and the filling is bubbly and cooked through.

Cool and Serve:
- Allow the Empanada Gallega to cool in the pan for at least 15-20 minutes before slicing and serving.
- Serve warm or at room temperature, optionally with a dollop of whipped cream or a scoop of vanilla ice cream for an extra indulgent treat.

Empanada Gallega is a delightful dessert that showcases the sweet and comforting flavors of apples, almonds, and spices, all wrapped in a tender and flaky crust. Enjoy this traditional Galician sweet pie with friends and family for a special occasion or as a delicious treat any time of year!

www.ingramcontent.com/pod-product-compliance
Lightning Source LLC
LaVergne TN
LVHW081601060526
838201LV00054B/2015